Preaching Through the Bible

Luke 1–11

Michael Eaton

Sovereign World

Sovereign World
PO Box 777
Tonbridge
Kent, TN11 0ZS
England

By the same author:
Ecclesiastes (Tyndale Commentary) – IVP
Living A Godly Life – Paternoster
Living Under Grace (Romans 6–7) – Paternoster
Enjoying God's Worldwide Church – Paternoster
No Condemnation – IVP (USA)
1 Samuel (Preaching Through the Bible) – Sovereign World
2 Samuel (Preaching Through the Bible) – Sovereign World
1, 2 Thessalonians (Preaching Through the Bible) – Sovereign World
Mark (Preaching Through the Bible) – Sovereign World
Genesis 1–11 (Preaching Through the Bible) – Sovereign World
1, 2, 3 John (Focus on the Bible) – Christian Focus
Hosea (Focus on the Bible) – Christian Focus
Genesis 12–13 (Preaching Through the Bible) – Sovereign World
1 Kings (Preaching Through the Bible) – Sovereign World
Joel and Amos (Preaching Through the Bible) – Sovereign World
Return to Glory (Romans 3:22–5:21) – Paternoster
1 Corinthians 1–9 (Preaching Through the Bible) – Sovereign World
1 Peter (Preaching Through the Bible) – Sovereign World
The Way That Leads to Life (Sermon on the Mount) – Christian Focus
Experiencing God Paternoster
Applying God's Law – Paternoster

ISBN: 1-85240-274-1

Typeset by CRB Associates, Reepham, Norfolk
Printed and bound in Great Britain by
Cox & Wyman Ltd, Reading, Berkshire

Preface

There is need of a series of biblical expositions which are especially appropriate for English-speaking people throughout the world. Such expositions need to be laid out in such a way that they will be useful to those who like to have their material, or (if they are preachers), to put across their material, in clear points. They need to avoid difficult vocabulary and advanced grammatical structures. They need to avoid European or North American illustrations. *Preaching Through the Bible* seeks to meet such a need. Although intended for an international audience, I have no doubt that their simplicity will be of interest to many first-language speakers of English as well. These expositions are based upon the Hebrew and Greek texts. The New American Standard Version and the New International Version of the Bible are recommended for the reader, but at times the expositor will simply translate the Hebrew or Greek himself. In this book quotations from Luke are from my own translation.

It is not our purpose to deal with minute exegetical detail, although the commentator has to do work of this nature as part of his preliminary preparation. But just as a housewife likes to serve a good meal rather than display her pots and pans, so we are concerned with the 'good meal' of Scripture, rather than the 'pots and pans' of dictionaries, disputed interpretations and the like. Only occasionally will such matters have to be discussed. Similarly matters of 'introduction' receive only as much attention as is necessary for the exposition to be clear. Although on the surface written simply, these expositions aim at a high level of scholarship, and attempt to put the theological and practical message of each book of the Bible in a clear and practical manner. On occasions a simple outline of some introductory matters will be included, perhaps in an appendix, but the first chapter of each exposition gets into the message of Scripture as speedily as possible.

Michael A. Eaton

Contents

Author's Preface

Until quite recently I had not preached very often on the Gospel of Luke. My preaching on the gospels has generally focused on Mark's Gospel or Matthew's Gospel. But in recent months and years I have turned my attention to Luke's Gospel. Friends in Nairobi have been hearing a lot of expositions on Luke's Gospel lately! I recall that the message on 'New Wine and New Wineskins' was the first message I preached at a time when Chrisco's 'City Church' felt they should become two congregations. Half the congregation went to a hall in the University of Nairobi while the other half stayed in Nairobi Cinema. I was simply preaching the Gospel of Luke, but on that Sunday we reached 'New Wine and New Wineskins' (see Chapter 25). 'God is always moving us on . . . God is likely to do something new at any moment . . . We go where the grace of God is leading us today!' It is surprising when you preach through books of the Bible – and when led that way by the Holy Spirit – how you are often in the right passage at the right time.

In this book I pay special attention to the relationship between the gospels. Readers interested in reading all four gospels side-by-side to get a picture of as much as we know of the life of Jesus should pay special attention to the paragraphs which outline the way the four gospels are moving through the story of Jesus (see the paragraphs at the beginning of Chapter 14 and others like it).

I am grateful to family and friends for their help, in different ways, in the work of seeing my preaching put into print. Our prayer is that our little book may help preachers.

Michael A. Eaton

If you enjoy this book and would like to help us to send a copy of it and many other titles to needy pastors in the **Third World**, please write for further information or send your gift to:

Sovereign World Trust
PO Box 777, Tonbridge
Kent TN11 0ZS
United Kingdom

or to the **'Sovereign World'** distributor in your country.

Visit our website at **www.sovereign-world.org** for a full range of Sovereign World books.

Chapter 1

Introducing Luke's Gospel

(Luke 1:1–4)

Luke begins with a long sentence of forty-two words (in Greek) explaining his qualifications for writing, his methods, his aim, and the circumstances in which he is doing his writing.

> *'Since many have undertaken to compile an account of the things that were accomplished among us* (1:1) *(in agreement with those who from the beginning were eyewitnesses and servants of the Word)* (1:2)*, it seemed fitting for me as well, having followed everything carefully from the beginning, to write it out for you in an orderly manner – most excellent Theophilus* (1:3) *– so that you might know the exact truth about the things you have been taught* (1:4).*'*

These words let us know a lot about how the gospels were written.

1. **The gospel of Jesus is about facts**. *'Since many have undertaken to compile an account of the things that were accomplished among us . . . '*. Certain events had taken place, and everyone knew about them. There were people who made known these basic facts, 'the things that were accomplished'.

2. **The gospel of Jesus is about momentous and significant events**. The word that Luke uses, 'accomplished', suggests that these great events were brought about by God. They were 'fulfilled' or 'accomplished'. God had said that He would do certain things, things that were impossible for men and women; the time came when He 'accomplished' them.

3. **The events of the life and death and resurrection of Jesus were well known to the early Christians**. Luke says they were things that happened 'among us'. The early Christians included people who had witnessed for themselves Jesus' death and resurrection and ascension, people like Mary, the mother of Jesus, and James, the brother of Jesus, and dozens more. They were some of the 120 people who had been present on the day of Pentecost.

4. **Luke had predecessors**. Others had written 'gospels' before Luke wrote this one. Many people had *'undertaken to compile an account of the things that were accomplished'*. The gospel of Jesus had **partly** been handed down orally, but there were **also** some written records. Some disciples may have taken notes of Jesus' teaching. So there were plenty of witnesses to the facts of the gospel. Luke refers not to two groups of people (that is, one group who were 'eyewitnesses' and another who were 'servants of the Word') but to one group who were both 'eyewitnesses and servants of the Word'. (i) Some people were eyewitnesses of the gospel but were not servants of the Word. They had seen what had happened but were not specially called to be preachers. (ii) Some people were servants of the Word but were not eyewitnesses. They had become preachers later but were not among the original group who had actually seen Jesus in His life and ministry and death and resurrection. (iii) Some people were neither eye-witnesses nor servants of the Word. They were neither preachers nor had they been present with the physically risen Jesus. (iv) Some people were **both** eyewitnesses of the risen Jesus **and** preachers of the Word of God. It was this small but well-informed and highly qualified group of people who were present at the beginning of the historical events of the Christian faith. They gave the next generation ('to us') the outline of the events that had taken place.

So Luke is joining a group of people who had already written accounts of what had happened. *'It seemed fitting for me as well . . . '* says Luke. Others had written gospels. He wants to write a gospel as well. Why should he want to write another one? He is not **criticising** his predecessors, but he feels that he has a contribution to make, and that he can add to what they have already done. Mark's Gospel was short. Luke had much more information and the Christians would benefit by having the extra material that Luke had. Matthew's Gospel was very Jewish; it was specially designed for Jews and it was laid out in a way that was intended to show Jews that Jesus was their Messiah, and to explain to Jews why and how it happened that the gospel was going out to the entire world.

Luke needed to write a gospel that included the extra information he had. It was designed for Gentiles and used the style of a Greek historian.

Luke tells us how he set about his work. He wrote *'having followed everything carefully from the beginning'*. The word 'follow' here means to observe closely, to investigate, to follow along with what has happened. Then Luke says he wrote out his material *'in an orderly manner'* It is mostly in chronological order. On the few occasions when it is out of order (such as in Luke 3:19–20), the material is being put in a section dealing with the same subject matter.

He says that he wrote for a high-born Christian, named Theophilus. *'It seemed fitting for me ... to write it out for you ... most excellent Theophilus'*. His purpose was that this man 'might know the exact truth about the things you have been taught.'

These claims of Luke in Luke 1:1–4 fit what is known about Luke from other sources. Luke is concerned to tell the facts about Jesus, showing that He is the One who brings salvation to the entire world.

Chapter 2

Fear Instead of Faith

(Luke 1:5–25)

Luke goes a long way back in the records connected with Jesus' birth and starts his story with an event that took place about a year before Jesus was born.

God sovereignly began to prepare for the coming of His Son. God began to move in the life of a few people in and around Jerusalem. It was the time of Herod the Great, who ruled over Israel between 40 BC and 4 BC. (The word 'Judea' in 1:5 refers not to the southern province of Judea, but to the whole land of the Jews, Israel.) Our story takes place round about 6 BC, a year before the birth of Jesus. (Jesus was not born in AD 1. There were some errors in the calculation of the years.) God was planning to bring a miracle-child to prepare the way for Jesus.

Often when God is about to use someone in an important life-long ministry there is something special about his birth. Perhaps the child is conceived with difficulty (think of Isaac or Samuel), or there is a special message at the time of the birth (think of Jacob or Samson), or there will be a special deliverance from danger (as in Matthew 2:13–14). The birth of John the Baptist, the son of Zacharias and Elizabeth, was announced by an angel.

God used a couple whose life had been a mixture of godliness and suffering. Zacharias and Elizabeth were elderly, perhaps in their sixties. They were from the priestly family of Aaron in the tribe of Levi. They were righteous people (1:6), but had also been through the great distress of having no children (1:7). They had long before prayed for a child (as 1:13) but had now given up hope. God uses those whose life has been a mixture of godliness and suffering. It seems that adversity and suffering have to come into our lives to drive us to God in a deeper way. One never meets a godly person without there having been some suffering in his or her life.

God answered a prayer unexpectedly. Twice a year priests had to do their duty at the temple in Jerusalem and Zacharias' turn had come (1:8). Before the morning sacrifice and after the evening sacrifice one of the priests had to go inside the 'holy place' and offer incense. The privilege of offering incense was experienced only once in a lifetime. Among the candidates (those who had not offered incense before) lots were cast to decide which one should have the privilege (1:9).

All of the furniture inside the 'holy place' of the temple symbolised fellowship with God. The incense stood for the fact that God was symbolically providing prayer for us. Our prayers get mixed with His provision and are acceptable to Him.

So here is Zacharias experiencing the once-in-a-lifetime event of offering up incense – a ceremony which speaks of the acceptability of our prayers to God. Suddenly an angel appears, standing at the very point of the symbolism which speaks of the acceptability of our prayers. The people are praying also (1:10–11). Will Zacharias think of the prayer that he might have a son? Actually his only reaction is to be afraid (1:12)!

How sad it is that sometimes when God is about to give us the greatest blessing of our life, we respond with fear! We all tend to be sinfully afraid of God. Of course there is a good and right 'fear of God' – an intense concern not to be chastised by Him. But there is also a sinful fear of God, an unwillingness to believe that He wants to be good and kind towards us. It is a fear that arises our of our feelings of guilt. When God appears in some way we tend to immediately think of our weaknesses and our past sinful ways. God sends an angel to give Zacharias the greatest answer to prayer ever in his life, but Zacharias responds with fear. Yet God is more gracious than Zacharias expected. The angel tells him his prayer for a child has been answered (1:13) and goes on to give a prophecy of the birth of John the Baptist (1:14–17).

Zacharias, however, is sceptical. How can that prayer be answered now? He and his wife are too old (1:18).

But the angel protests (1:19). He is an angel. He stands day and night in the presence of God! But Zacharias wants to be sceptical. Sometimes we can get so unbelieving that if an angel were to appear to us we would start arguing! This is Gabriel, the same angel who appeared to Daniel and gave predictions about the kingdom of God (Daniel 8:16; 9:21). Zacharias is questioning the possibility of the miraculous and is arguing with an angel. This shows us the great power of unbelief. Zacharias is a godly man and he has been asking God to do something wonderful for him. Now he is talking to an angel but still will not believe the prayer he prayed will be answered – even though the angel is standing next to the incense altar which speaks of the acceptability of our prayers!

God does not like it when we are unready for prayer to be answered. Zacharias is rebuked. He will be dumb and deaf (as 1:62 implies) until John is born (1:20–22).

It happened as the angel said. The couple went back home (1:23). Elizabeth became pregnant (1:24–25). Zacharias' disabilities were not permanent. A day of rejoicing came eventually (1:57–64). But it was enough to teach everyone who knew Zacharias that God wants us to be ready for the answer to our praying. If our prayer is sinful we stop praying. If God says 'No' we stop praying. Otherwise we go on believing that God's promises 'will be fulfilled in their proper time.'

Chapter 3

John the Baptist

(Luke 1:15–17)

The angel told Zacharias about his child to be born whose name would be John (1:14–17).

> *'For he shall be great before the Lord, and wine and fermented drink he shall not take; and he will be filled with the Holy Spirit even from his mother's womb. And many of the people of Israel he will bring back to the Lord their God. And he will go on before Him in the spirit and power of Elijah, to turn the hearts of the fathers to their children and the disobedient to the wisdom of the righteous, to make ready a people prepared for the Lord.'*
>
> (Luke 1:15–17)

John the Baptist was a very great man. *'He shall be great before the Lord'*, said the angel. Not only would Zacharias and Elizabeth rejoice to have their prayers answered, many people would thank God that John the Baptist had been born. *'And you shall have joy and exultation . . . '* said the angel, *'and many will rejoice over his birth'* (1:14). John the Baptist would bring many people to repentance; many would rejoice because he had brought them to know God.

They would rejoice because of the greatness of John's ministry. *'For he shall be great before the Lord'* (1:15). But what is greatness? Is it wealth? Is it popularity? An easy life? Greatness is living for God and achieving something for God.

1. **John's unusual life would require unusual discipline**. He would be called to avoid the weak diluted wine that was generally used by the people of Jesus' day. Jesus' first miracle

involved making hundreds of litres of this diluted wine, but John's ministry would require the total avoidance of any kind of wine. *'For he shall be great before the Lord, and wine and fermented drink he shall not take . . . '*. Some believers are called to go beyond others in their discipline or their abstinence from the ordinary blessings of life.

2. **John's ministry would involve the power of the Holy Spirit**. It was a very unusual blessing for John when it was said *'. . . and he will be filled with the Holy Spirit even from his mother's womb'*. John seems to have come to salvation in the womb. He was born believing! This seems to be entirely unique in the story of the Bible. It certainly teaches us that the Holy Spirit is totally sovereign in the way He does things. From the earliest days John grew up conscious of the power of the Holy Spirit upon him.

The Holy Spirit is never totally within our control. No one can 'switch on' the gift of the Holy Spirit. Even Jesus waited thirty years before He received the Spirit. The Spirit can be asked for in faith but you are never entirely in control.

The great proof of the sovereignty of the Spirit in this matter is John the Baptist. He knew the power of the Spirit from infancy!

3. **John had an 'Elijah ministry'**. He would have *'the spirit and power of Elijah'*. He would bring spiritual awakening to Judea, and this would overcome the barriers between children and their fathers. He would *'turn the hearts of the fathers to their children'*. It would overcome the barrier between ungodliness and godliness in the land. He would turn *'the disobedient to the wisdom of the righteous'*. Elijah was able to swing an entire nation around for God. John had a similar calling. Some people have this special ministry. John would one day preach in the desert of Judea not far from Jerusalem. Hundreds of people would come under conviction and would seek forgiveness from God. John was able to bring thousands of the common people out of spiritual deadness and formality into liveliness and eagerness for the coming of the Messiah, Jesus.

4. **Spiritual power consists of being able to bring people to repentance**. John was a 'charismatic' even before he was born

(see 1:44)! But what did his power consist of? Healings? Prophecies? Miracles? No, none of these things. But he was able to bring men and women to a conviction of sin. He was able to bring them to repentance. Even Pharisees would come seeking forgiveness from God. One has to have spiritual power to convict Pharisees! Yet John would be able to touch hardened fathers, backslidden children, soldiers, Pharisees, religious people, and wicked people.

5. **The mark of John's revival was that it bridged the generations**. When there is spiritual backsliding, the fathers and the children become distant from each other. Spiritual awakening changes that. This is one of the marks of spiritual revival. All ages are reached with the preaching of God's Word. In times of spiritual decline the churches reach only women and children. Certain types of preaching only reach intellectuals, and yet those intellectuals do nothing for God. But when God is moving powerfully every kind of person is touched, and it would be this way in the ministry of John the Baptist.

6. **John had a ministry of preparation**. He would lead a great spiritual movement but it would be only the beginning of what God was about to do. He would bring into being a 'people prepared'. Then some months after the spiritual awakening led by John the Baptist, Jesus Himself would come. Jesus would have only a short ministry of just over three years. Yet the people were ready for Jesus to come. They had been prepared by John. Sometimes there is a preparatory movement of the Spirit before God works in great blessing. We do not have to prepare ourselves to believe in Jesus. Not at all! But in movements of revival God often does a work of preparation. One movement of the Holy Spirit is followed by something yet greater. John was followed by Jesus.

Chapter 4

The Greatest Day of Mary's Life

(Luke 1:26–38)

Do you ever wonder when will be the greatest moment of your life? Was it a long time ago in your younger days? Or will your greatest moment be in your advanced years (as it was with Zacharias and Elizabeth)? This event in Luke 1:26–38 was undoubtedly the greatest moment in the story of Mary, the mother of Jesus.

1. **God's mighty acts always catch us by surprise**. Look at Mary. This event certainly caught her by surprise. She was young, probably somewhere between fifteen and twenty years old. She was a spiritual person. She also had the kind of ordinary plans that any girl in her late teens might have. She was betrothed to a young man by the name of Joseph.

Suddenly God stepped into her life and did something entirely dramatic. An angel appears to her. One of the greatest of the angels, Gabriel, comes to tell her something from God.

In Mary's life the natural and the supernatural are side-by-side. She is a perfectly natural young lady. She is not a nun living in a convent. She is a teenager happily in love with a spiritual man named Joseph. And yet alongside a perfectly natural lifestyle comes a visitation from an angel!

The Christian life is like this. The natural and the supernatural run together side by side. We are ordinary people in many ways. We have perfectly natural desires and inclinations. Yet alongside the natural, there is the supernatural. God is in our lives and He might do something special at any moment. At any moment the supernatural might break through.

It was not only a surprise in the life of Mary, it was also a surprise in the history of the world. God is about to send His

Son. He chooses a despised country – Israel. He chooses a despised area of that country – Galilee. He chooses an unimportant village within that area – Nazareth (1:26). He chooses not a famous rich man or a mighty politician, but an obscure teenage girl (1:27). However, the teenage girl is engaged to someone in the house of David whose ancestors were kings of Israel.

There was a promise in the Old Testament that although the kings in the line of David had ceased to function, yet God was still watching over the royal line. One day, it was promised, God's royal Saviour would come out of the line of David. At the time of our story the line of David was humiliated and despised. It did not seem very likely that any kings would be coming from it just yet! In any case the kind of 'Son of David' that people were hoping for was a soldier-politician who would reverse the fortunes of Israel and drive out the occupying Roman armies.

God used a surprising country, a surprising area, a surprising town, a surprising girl. And He used a surprising method: a miraculous birth!

2. **God's mighty acts open up great privileges**. The angel greets Mary: *'Greetings, you highly favoured person, the Lord is with you'* (1:28). Mary is amazed (1:29). What sort of greeting is this? She is afraid at being in the presence of an angel (1:30). She has sins and weaknesses in her life as much as anyone else. Any human being is afraid when God draws near to us, because we have somewhat guilty consciences. Even when we have been forgiven the memory of how weak and sinful we have been can at any moment come back to us – especially when we are talking to an angel! But the angel encourages her. *'Don't be afraid'* (1:30), he says. And Mary is told what is about to happen. She will supernaturally give birth to God's Saviour (1:31–33). No sexual relationship with any man will be involved (1:34–35). God is doing something new in the story of the world. He has already started the process and Elizabeth is also expecting her son to be born (1:36–37).

Jesus is about to be supernaturally born. A man is going to come into the world who is genuinely human but who has no earthly Father. He will be a Second Adam, a second person in the story of the human race who has no father but God. Like Adam, Jesus will be a person who comes into this world without sin. With Him, God will start the human race again.

3. **God's chosen instruments experience suffering**. It might seem a great privilege for Mary to give birth to Jesus, and yet what suffering was involved. Who would believe her when she said her pregnancy was miraculous. Who would understand? It would be quite impossible for her to explain. It would be decades before there was any group of people who would believe her. I suppose that it was not until after the day of Pentecost that there would be any large group of people who would believe her story.

And what suffering she would go through, seeing her Son despised and rejected and eventually crucified. God's servants invariably have tough times. They have to abandon all hopes of being understood by anyone. Nor will they ever be understood. Jesus was never understood. No promise exists that they must be vindicated during their own lifetime.

4. **God's chosen instruments have to leave themselves in the hands of God**. Mary replied: *'Look at me, the servant-girl of the Lord. Let it be the way you have said'*. She accepts God's call for her life. She is willing to let God do to her and through her whatever He wants.

The day God calls us, the day we let God do whatever He wants, it will turn out to be the greatest day of our lives.

Chapter 5

The People of the Holy Spirit

(Luke 1:39–45)

Mary has been told of the miraculous birth that is about to take place through her. She has expressed her willingness that this should happen, and the angel has let her know that Elizabeth and Zacharias are involved in what God is doing.

1. **It is good to have fellowship with a believing friend**. Mary goes from Nazareth to a city in Judah, about 80–100 miles away (1:39). It is uncertain which 'town of Judah' is the one in which Elizabeth lived. Mary wants to share her news and pray with her believing friend. John the Baptist and Jesus were part of the same forward movement of God in the history of the world. Their mothers want to pray together.

It is good to have fellowship with other believers. When they are humble, unpretentious, full of faith and of praise, it is a great help to us to talk to them and pray with them. In the days of Malachi, *'those who feared the Lord, talked to one another'*. It was specially pleasing to God. *'The Lord gave attention and heard it'* (Malachi 3:16).

2. **The meeting between Mary and Elizabeth was an occasion when the Spirit came down with power upon the two friends**. Mary arrives at Elizabeth's home and greets her (1:40). As she does so Elizabeth feels a forceful movement within her womb (1:41), and at that very point she receives a special filling with the Holy Spirit! God is full of wonders and surprises! There are more things in heaven and on earth than our philosophy ever dreams of! God can give physical manifestations of His presence. He can give fresh fillings of the Spirit to His people at any point. He can fill a baby with the Holy Spirit before the baby is born!

In this particular instance the filling of the Holy Spirit gives a special enabling for worship. The term 'fill' or 'filling' or 'full' of the Holy Spirit may mean different things at different times in the Bible. The term 'filling' of the Holy Spirit is not the same as the baptism with the Spirit. The word is generally used quite differently.

(i) Sometimes it refers to a special enabling (as in Exodus 31:3). In the early chapters of Luke there are several occasions when people are given special enablings by God (see Luke 1:41, 67). On the day of Pentecost people were 'filled' in order to be able to speak in tongues (Acts 2:4). Peter was specially 'filled' with the Spirit to be able to reply to the persecuting authorities in Jerusalem (Acts 4:8). Something similar happens in Acts 4:31; 13:9.

(ii) There is **another** use of the term where it refers to a constant readiness to live for God. This is what is involved when we are told to 'go on being filled with the Holy Spirit' (Ephesians 5:18) and when people are described as being 'full' of the Holy Spirit (see Luke 4:1; Acts 6:3; 7:55; 11:24; 13:52). Sometimes it is hard to known whether something continuous or something special is being referred to (as in Luke 1:15; Acts 7:55).

Here there can be little doubt. A special enabling came upon Mary in which she was specially enabled to lift up her voice in inspired song and worship. The 'filling' was a special enabling of the Holy Spirit. In this story, it was connected with the ability to worship and praise God in an inspired way.

3. **The new events in the kingdom of God were introduced with music, worship, and boldness of speech**. This is the way it often is in God's kingdom. The kingdom of God is righteousness, peace and joy in the Holy Spirit. When God is doing something new there is always 'joy in the Holy Spirit'! It always produces new songs. Every revival, every forward step, in the kingdom of God produces new songs. 'He has put a new song in my mouth' is what the people of God say, every time He specially blesses them. Here Elizabeth is emotional and deeply moved at what is happening. She cries out with a loud voice (1:42). She congratulates Mary in the power of the Holy Spirit (1:42). She has special revelation and insight. She

knows that Mary's baby will be *'my Lord'* (1:43). When, it might be asked, did people first realise that Jesus would be the Messiah? Elizabeth knew even before He was born!

People who are not very conspicuous sometimes turn out to know a lot about the Holy Spirit. These people in the early chapters of Luke are humble, inconspicuous people. No one knew about them in Jerusalem. They are quietly *'righteous in the sight of God'* (1:6). God is with them (1:28). They worship regularly at the temple (1:9). They know their Old Testament extremely well. Their very language is full of the Old Testament. Mary's song in Luke 1:46–55 is full of echoes of Hannah's song in 1 Samuel chapter 1. The world knew nothing about them but angels come to visit them!

It is in this humble atmosphere that the Holy Spirit is powerfully at work. The Holy Spirit is the one who will produce Mary's miracle child (1:35). The Holy Spirit gives them insight. Sometimes their words are full of prophetic insight. Five times in this first chapter we have reference to the Holy Spirit (1:15, 17, 35, 41, 67). Here are people who have not reached the day of Pentecost. Yet they know much of the Holy Spirit already! They have clear spiritual knowledge. Above all, they are people who know what it means to have faith in the promises of God. *'Blessed is she who believed that there would be a fulfilment of what had been spoken to her by the Lord'* (1:45).

Chapter 6

Mary's Song

(Luke 1:46–56)

Mary has been blessed by God. It leads immediately to worship and praise.

1. **Mary's song is full of joy**. She wants to lift God high in joyful admiration. *'My soul exalts the Lord, and my spirit has rejoiced in God my Saviour'* (1:47).

When God moves in our lives, it leads to outpourings of the Holy Spirit. And outpourings of the Holy Spirit always lead to joy, and joy in the Holy Spirit leads to singing and worship.

2. **Mary is filled with a sense of privilege and amazement that God should use her**. *'He has regarded the humble situation of his servant. From this time onwards all generations will call me blessed'* (1:48).

God's people know that any blessing that has come to them has been entirely of God's mercy. Mary attributes what has happened to God: *'He has regarded ... His servant'*. She knows it is not her doing at all.

3. **Mary is moved at the way God exalts poor and despised people**. This is a theme of Luke's Gospel. God favours lowliness (1:48), scatters proud people (1:51), reduces the powerful to weakness (1:52), sends rich people away empty-handed (1:53).

What amazes Mary is God's goodness to her despite her humble situation. Mary was not a rich person. We often think that the only people who are used by God are the clever, the rich, those who come from notable families, or who have been educated in famous places. None of these things are necessary. When God is doing big things He tends to use despised people.

4. **She is moved at the greatness of what God has done**. When God decided to act the world hardly notices, and yet He does great and mighty things. Soon the greatness of what God has done is discovered, but people like Mary are in at the beginning. *'For the Mighty One has done great things for me; and holy is His name'* (1:49).

5. **The great things God does, lead us to see His character**. Mary is praising God for His great and wonderful character. He is 'the Mighty One'. His name is holy. He always does things in a pure and holy manner.

> *'And His mercy is upon generation after generation, for those who fear Him. He has done mighty deeds with His arm; He has scattered the proud in the thoughts of their hearts.'* (Luke 1:50–51)

She sees how merciful and tender God is. The nation of Israel is at its worst! An unconverted high-priest followed by spiritually decayed priests and rabbis are the leaders of the land. There are not many people like Zacharias. Roman armies rule the nation. Yet unexpectedly God is having mercy. At a time when Israel seems to be totally abandoned by God, God is sending His Saviour. How unexpected it is! How merciful! How it upsets the thoughts and expectations of clever people!

6. **She realises that God's ways are so unexpected**. She realises that God is fulfilling His promises to the house of David. *'He has brought down rulers from their thrones, and has exalted those who were humble'* (1:52).

Mary is thinking of the line of kings that descended from David. More than five centuries previously God had brought the proud rulers in the line of King David to an end. The kings of Judah in previous centuries had abandoned the godliness of their ancestor David and had turned to idolatry. God *'brought down rulers from their thrones'* and ended the kings of Judah. But the line of king David has been preserved, and now God is taking a humble girl and raising up another 'Son of David'. Mary continues her singing concerning God's habit of humiliating the proud and raising the humble.

'He has filled the hungry with good things, and He has sent the rich away empty. He has helped His servant Israel, in remembrance of His mercy, as He spoke to our forefathers, to Abraham and his seed for ever.' (Luke 1:53–55)

7. **She realises that God is fulfilling His promises in the Scriptures**. He had sworn to Abraham centuries before that out of his seed would come someone who would be a blessing to all the nations of the world. Mary is lifted up by the Holy Spirit to see that it is at this time and through her body that God is about to fulfil His promise.

8. **She views her life in the light of the purpose of God**. Mary's worship is not self-centred. Although she has a sense of privilege, what is stirring her heart is the thought that she is playing a part in the kingdom of God.

Mary was a great woman. She was not conceived without sin as some think. There is not a scrap of teaching in the Bible about that! On the contrary, Mary knows that she needs a Saviour. She worships 'God my Saviour'. She is a sinner as everyone else is. Only Jesus came into this world without sin. Mary was not without sin, but she was a great woman of faith.

When God blesses us there is a little context and a big context at the same time. What I mean is: He blesses us personally with amazing privileges, but at the same time He takes forward steps in His kingdom. Mary was amazed that God should use her. What was more amazing was that a forward step was being taken: God was sending His Son into the world.

Chapter 7

Mercy After Chastening

(Luke 1:57–66)

Zacharias had been severely chastened for his unbelief. For many months he had been unable to speak (1:20, 22) and unable to hear (as 1:62 suggests). He had been living in a world where he was cut off from people and had much time to think over what had happened.

1. **The purposes of God for our lives are not easily aborted**. One might think that because of his unbelief, God would abandon Zacharias and withdraw His prediction that John the Baptist should be his son. But God does not withdraw His plans easily and lightly. He does not deal with us as our sins deserve. The great privilege that was being given to Zacharias was not withdrawn. The angel had insisted that his words would be fulfilled despite Zacharias' unbelief (1:20).

So in due course Elizabeth gives birth to a son (1:57). For five months she had kept her pregnancy secret (1:25), but then after Mary's visit in the sixth month she felt free to share her news. Her friends and relatives rejoiced over what had happened (1:58). People were rejoicing but Zacharias was shut out of the celebrations because of his deaf and dumb condition.

2. **The chastening of God does not go on for ever**. When God expresses His displeasure it may feel as if He has abandoned us for ever. Zacharias must have had many long and lonely months cut off from the joys and pleasures involved in anticipating the birth of his son. But the chastening of God does not go on for ever.

The child was born and after eight days the normal custom of circumcising the boy was about to take place. The name was to be given at the same time and it was taken for granted by everyone that he would be named after his father (1:59), but Elizabeth insisted it was to be 'John' (1:60), as the angel had said (1:13). The name is Johanan; 'John' is the common English form. It means 'The Lord has shown favour'. The birth of John was a sign of great mercy to his parents, but it was also the beginning of the time when God was showing mercy to the world in the sending of Jesus. John would prepare the way. 'The LORD has shown favour' was the name of the person who would go ahead of Jesus, God's Son.

The name suggested by Elizabeth evidently causes a lot of surprise and even some disapproval. Surely the child should be named after his father or after a member of the family (1:61). They call for Zacharias and despite his impediments they are able to explain what is happening and ask his opinion (1:62). He asks for a writing tablet and, to everyone's surprise, insists that the name should be John.

3. **God's chastening ends at the point where we have learned what God wants to teach us**. At the point where he insists that the name should be John, he can speak! The point where the chastening ends should be noted. He has had many months in which he could do little but pray. Now he firmly resists attempts from his family to give his son a different name. He is now determined to respond to the angel's instruction concerning the name (see 1:13). He is obeying the angel with the obedience of faith. He does not want to take the risk of displeasing God any further. It is to this point that God has been wanting to bring him. When he expresses his obedience to what he knows is God's will concerning the name, at that point the chastening ends.

4. **Zacharias' new obedience brings him fresh joy**. As soon as he can speak he begins to praise God! Despite the months of solitude he has no criticism of God. He has learned much and is now ready to acknowledge that God has been dealing with him. His mouth is opened and for the first time he is able to speak of what happened in the temple (1:64). He immediately praises God and tells everyone what has happened. It leads to a respect for God and His ways coming upon the people who hear Zacharias' story (1:65). It stirs the hearts of the people all

around the area and they begin to expect that something special is about to take place through this child (1:66). From the very moment he is born the hand of the Lord is upon John. There is widespread publicity concerning what has happened. John grows up from his earlier days under the care and direction of God.

John had a special work to do for God. The greater the task that God wants us to fulfil, the greater will be the early workings of God in our lives. John had a very special work to do. There would be much suffering in it. The hand of the Lord was upon him but this would not stop his being arrested later on in his life. Eventually he would be murdered by Herod Antipas. Yet none of this prevented him from completing his life's work. He had a special work to do for God and God made it clear in the very circumstances of his birth. The last phrase of verse 66 is seemingly part of the people's comment. The people could see that the Lord was working powerfully through John, Zacharias' son.

The whole story is typical of what happens when God moves suddenly and powerfully. God is sovereign. He is a mighty king and when His people are in weakness He can act unexpectedly and powerfully. This is the way it was when Jesus was about to come into the world. God began to get people ready. Zacharias' chastening was the prelude to God's working in new and wonderful ways.

Chapter 8

A Song from the Holy Spirit

(Luke 1:67–80)

There are three songs given by the Holy Spirit in the early chapters of Luke. We have had one from Mary (1:46–55). There will be another one from Simon (2:29–32). At this point we have one from Zacharias. Zacharias was suddenly given a special enabling by the Holy Spirit (1:46), leading him to 'prophesy', that is, to speak with words being given to him by God. Verses 68 to 75 are one long sentence.

1. **First, Zacharias praised God for the realisation that the day of salvation had begun**. It will be noticed that the song does not begin by saying much about Zacharias' new baby son! It is more about God and what He is doing. Zacharias knows that Mary's child is even more important than his own child. *'Blessed be the Lord, the God of Israel, for He has visited and redeemed His people'* (1:68).

God has come to save His people! Zacharias uses the past tense. Actually what God was doing through Jesus was only beginning but in Zacharias' mind it is as good as done! He uses a past tense; it is a well-known Hebrew way of speaking about something that is so certain it is as good as done! *'. . . and He has raised up a horn of salvation for us in the house of David His servant . . .'* (1:69).

The 'horn' of an animal was famous for its strength and power. A 'horn of salvation' means 'a powerful salvation'. God is fulfilling His promises. He had promised a Saviour in the line of David, and now Zacharias knows God's promise is being fulfilled. God is acting *'. . . as He spoke by the mouth of His holy prophets long ago . . .'* (1:70). For many centuries, godly people have been living on what God had predicted. Now it is about to take place.

2. Next, **Zacharias describes what he expects this salvation to be**. It will involve rescue from enemies: *'... that we should be saved from our enemies, and from the hand of all that hate us ...'* (1:71).

Men and women have many enemies. Israel was oppressed by the Romans at the time when Jesus was born, and so there was not much possibility of that society fulfilling the will of God in its national life. But it was not just a political problem. Men and women face a mass of adversaries and adversities, spiritual and not-so-spiritual. Sin is an enemy; Satan is an enemy. The ill-will and cruelty of people around us can be fierce. But Zacharias knew God's salvation would change all this. It puts us right with God and then we are in a position to cope with everything else. Eventually it even transforms society.

God's intervention was sheer mercy. Jesus and His forerunner John come because God is showing mercy. *'... to bring about the mercy promised to our fathers, and to remember His holy covenant ...'* (1:72).

Long before God had promised mercy to Israel, and through Israel to the world. It had all begun with Abraham. *'... the oath which He swore to our father Abraham ...'* (1:73). It is notable that Zacharias refers specially to God's oath in Genesis 22:16–18. God's 'oath' is a promise that cannot be lost.

Another aspect of this salvation is rescue, deliverance from any kind of oppression. *'... to grant us to be delivered from the hand of our enemies'* (1:74).

And God promises fearlessness, *'... so that we might serve Him without fear ...'* (1:75a).

Everything leads to godly living before God, *'in holiness and righteousness before Him all the days of our life'* (1:75a).

3. Next, **Zacharias rejoices in the part that his own son would have in introducing God's salvation**. Like John himself, Zacharias knows that John's only task is to introduce Jesus:

'And you child, will be called the prophet of the Most High, for you will go before the Lord to prepare His ways.'
(Luke 1:76)

This is what every prophet and preacher does. He 'prepares' the way for God. The person is not called upon to prepare himself. The sinners task is not to prepare himself, but to believe! Yet the preacher or prophet often clears things out of the way. He gives the preliminary knowledge that is needed for anyone to believe in Jesus. God wanted someone to make it clear that Jesus was not a politician or soldier, but a Saviour from sin. John would start to make the message clear even before Jesus came.

'In the Holy Spirit' Zacharias sees all of this. He knows Jesus comes: *'to give knowledge of salvation to His people, through the forgiveness of their sins . . . '* (1:77).

Salvation is first of all forgiveness. Everything starts with being reconciled to God. Then we are ready to have our prayers answered, and to serve God. Then we shall have an influence on others around us.

Forgiveness is first, *'through the tender mercy of our God when the dawn from on high shall rise upon us . . . '* (1:78).

Salvation is not simply religious routine. It is a person. Salvation comes when Jesus comes. He was like the sun rising in a dark place. When He comes all is light and brightness. He comes like the sun, *'. . . to shine upon those who sit in darkness and upon those in the shadow of death, to guide our feet into the way of peace'* (1:79).

Zacharias has a clear grasp of what the coming of Jesus will mean. He will bring forgiveness, illumination, guidance, peace.

John the Baptist grew physically and spiritually. He lived in an isolated region, until the time came in his life, when his public ministry began and all Israel got to know about him (1:80).

The Spirit can give marvellously clear knowledge. It is very early days in the events of the gospel, yet by the Spirit Zacharias sees it all.

Chapter 9

The Birth of Jesus

(Luke 2:1–11)

Luke presents us with a selection of stories coming from the time of Jesus' infancy. He has told us of the announcement of John's birth and the announcement of Jesus' birth, the visit of Mary to Elizabeth and the birth of John. Now there comes a fifth story. In a few verses we are told of the birth of Jesus.

1. **Luke has a special interest in history**. We can see this partly in the way he presents stories and lets them speak for themselves, but also he emphasises the dates of certain key events. The story he is about to tell took place in the days of Caesar Augustus (2:1), at a time of a census when Quirinius was governor (2:2). The mention of the Roman officials is Luke's way of locating the event in history.

2. **God's rule of the world ensures that prophecy is fulfilled**. Luke is specially drawing attention to the fact that Jesus is to be born in the house of David (1:27, 32, 69), in fulfilment of God's promises. The prophecy of Daniel also foretold that God's kingdom would be set up in a time of a 'fourth empire'. In Daniel's own lifetime the Babylonian empire came to an end, and the Medo-Persian empire began. After his death there would be the Greek empire. Then there would be a fourth empire; it turned out to be the Roman rule. Micah 5:2 predicted that Israel's ruler should come from Bethlehem.

Quirinius was a Roman official during AD 6–9, and there was a census in AD 6, when the emperor Augustus reduced Judea to a Roman province. But this is not the census that Luke has in mind here. Possibly Luke 2:2 should be translated 'This enrolment was **before** that made when Quirinius was governor of Syria . . . '. Or if the traditional translation is right

('This enrolment was **the first**...') it must refer to something that happened in about 4 BC. There were various censuses during Augustus' rule. Tertullian said there was one in Judea in the days when a Roman official Saturninus was ruling Judea.[1] Since Saturninus' work in Judea finished in 6 BC it is likely that Quirinius his successor took over the work and the census was being completed during about 4 BC when Jesus was born. Luke seems to mean that the work of registering the citizens of the empire was at that time being extended to Judea.

What is certain is that it was Roman rule that brought Mary to Bethlehem in fulfilment of Micah 5:5. In the midst of the 'fourth kingdom' God was setting up His kingdom!

3. **God's plan gets fulfilled in some surprising ways, often amidst sufferings and troubles**. What happened to Mary and Joseph was not pleasant. Mary was nine months pregnant. She had no choice but to go to Bethlehem (2:3–5). It was not easy for her to travel when she was just about to give birth. When they arrive there are hundreds of people who have also had to go to Bethlehem for the same reason at the same time. There is no room for them anywhere. There was no room for them in the local lodging. There would have been stables for the asses, camels and oxen. Finally they have to make use of one of these. Jesus was born and was allowed to sleep in a 'manger', a large feeding-place, which was (one imagines) made clean enough for Mary to use. There were no special clothes prepared for Him. There were no relatives and friends nearby. Mary had to wrap the baby herself. The situation was obviously difficult. Jesus has to be wrapped in some pieces of cloth that happened to be available (2:6–7).

God gets His will done in an amazing way. It gives no glory to any man or woman. Jesus was not born in a palace with admiring attendants and servants. Mary was not some beauty queen whose daily activities were reported to the world. But amidst many troubles and tribulations the plan of God was going forward. There was a kind of publicity. In a lodging place crowded with travellers everyone must have heard about the baby who had been born in the stable where the animals were kept. But it was not the kind of publicity that anyone would have wanted.

The first admirers of the new baby were shepherds! Jesus was born in a surprising country – despised Israel. He was born in surprising circumstances. Mary was not the kind of person you would expect God's Saviour to come from. She was an obscure girl living in despised Nazareth. The method which God used to introduce His Saviour was startling and unexpected. And it was announced first to shepherds of all people! Nearby in the open fields around Bethlehem were shepherds looking after their sheep. Rulers and kings were unaware of what was happening. Historians and writers were kept uninformed. No one told the Roman governor. The high-priest was not let in on the secret. The scribes and Pharisees had no idea of what was happening. But shepherds were visited by angels to be told the news! *'Has not God chosen the poor ... to be rich in faith and heirs of the kingdom ... ?'* (James 2:5).

4. **The angels come to mark out a great occasion in God's plan**. Whenever God does something highly significant, angels come to attend the occasion. It is a sign that Jesus is no ordinary baby. He is a real human being, yet He is 'the Lord' whose way John the Baptist prepares (1:16, 17, 76). He is 'Son of the Most High' (1:33), the 'Son of God' (1:35). Now the shepherds are told: He is 'a Saviour, Christ the Lord'. He is 'good news', a Saviour for everyone who will have Him.

Note

1. Tertullian, *Adversus Marcionem* 4:19.

Chapter 10

The Angels and the Shepherds

(Luke 2:8–20)

People who spent their time looking after animals were not thought to be very important. Shepherds could not keep ceremonially clean and please the orthodox Pharisees. They spent their time in the countryside. Rural people everywhere seem to be regarded as somehow beneath their city-dwelling contemporaries.

1. **Luke lets us know that God honours the underprivileged**. God chooses such people to hear the first news of the birth of His Son. Luke likes to point out how God chooses the despised people of the world. Luke made this point before by including Mary's song which insists that God favours lowliness (1:48), scatters proud people (1:51), reduces the powerful to weakness (1:52), sends rich people away empty-handed (1:53).

For the shepherds it comes as a great surprise. They are simply doing their usual work (2:8) when an angel appears to them. With the angel comes the radiating light of the glory of God (2:9).

2. **The attendance of angels lets us know that it was a special occasion in the plans of God**. God is entering the human race in a unique way. The coming of the angels begins with an appearance of one angel. As usual when an angel appears they respond with fear (2:9). It is natural for sinners to be afraid of God, so conscious are we of our sins. But although the fear of God in this way is natural God does not in fact want us to be afraid. Many times people who specially are drawn close to God are told not to fear (2:10).

3. **Salvation is being brought to the human race**. The

shepherds are told they need not fear, but should be rejoicing. A message of joy is on offer for everyone. It is for the entire human race (2:10b), and so it is for them ('to you', 2:11). It fulfils prophecy since the child is born in the city of David (2:11b). Anyone who is not rejoicing has failed to grasp the gospel message. It is about forgiveness and reconciliation with God.

The event is a step in God's bringing salvation. Every other message is essentially a message of what we must do and so is not really a joyful message. Who can rejoice at a programme of endeavours laid upon us? But this is not a message of what we must do. Rather it is a message of what God is doing and has done.

The angels spell out the content of the good news. God becoming man! A miraculous birth! A 'Saviour' (2:12) has come, One who will bring deliverance from the guilt and power of sin in their lives and from its numerous consequences. The child is 'Christ Lord' as the Greek has it (2:12), in an unusual phrase. We translate it 'Christ and Lord' or 'Christ the Lord'. The idea is that Jesus is a divine Messiah. The divine glory has come into the world.

4. **Salvation is offered to all but invites a response**. The shepherds are invited to believe what the angel says. The sign that they have found the child will be when they find a child wrapped in simple strips of cloth and lying in the eating-trough for animals (2:13). The city of Bethlehem will not have many lodging places. They must go to look for the child.

After the angel has spoken he is joined by a great multitude of angels praising God (2:13). *'Glory to God!'* they sing (2:14). It is a short phrase but it means 'God be honoured, because we see what He is like in what He has done!' God's power and mercy, God's amazingly surprising ways, are obvious in the amazing event that has taken place.

If in heaven God gets honour, on earth men are to get peace, because of the birth of the Christ-child. It will not be a man-centred peace or the peace of an easy life, but peace through being reconciled with God. It is peace 'among people of who are the objects of God's good pleasure'. The last phrase is interpreted differently by different people. (i) The old translation 'goodwill towards men' is not quite right, and translates inferior Greek manuscripts. (ii) It could be taken to mean 'people of goodwill', that is, those who respond to what God is giving them in Jesus. But the Greek word refers to God's pleasure, not human 'good will'. (iii) Rather it refers to the whole human race to whom God is pleased to give the Saviour – 'people whom God is pleased to bless'. It has the idea that Jesus is offered to everyone, and God would be pleased if everyone received Him.

The angels come because they accompany the events that take place in the life of Jesus. Angels appear with radiating glory only when they are representing God's special presence. The angels and the glory are the usual accompaniments of the appearing of God – but where is God? One almost expects a special appearing like that in Exodus 3:2–6, and elsewhere. God appears in the child. The child is the divine Messiah! It is His angels and His glory that has become visible to the shepherds.

After sharing their message and giving their choral fanfare with the shepherds, the angels withdraw (2:15) and the shepherds are left alone. They respond with faith, searching the lodging places of Bethlehem until they find the baby that has been described to them (2:16). Then they start telling everyone (2:17). New-found salvation cannot be kept quiet for long! The shepherds make known what has happened. Whom do they tell? Everyone they meet! The birth of Jesus requires a response. We should accept it as something amazing (2:18; with which we may compare 1:21, 63; 2:33). We should react with thoughtful submission, as Mary did (2:19). Like the shepherds we go on our way praising and glorifying God (2:20).

Chapter 11

Born Under the Law

(Luke 2:21–35)

The first thing that we are told from the events in Jesus' life is that He was circumcised on the eighth day after He was born (2:21).

1. **Jesus was born 'under the law'**. Circumcision began in the life of Abraham. For Abraham it was a sign of newness of life, a seal of his being reckoned righteous in the eyes of God. Later on it was required in the law of Moses for every Jewish boy, so it was a mark of Jewish nationality. In the life of Jesus it was a sign that He was being brought up as a loyal Jew. From the very earliest days of His life He was 'under the law' (as Paul put it in Galatians 4:5).

If Jesus was to be our Saviour He had Himself to be sinless, totally obedient to God. If the righteousness of Jesus was to be reckoned as ours, then Jesus had to live a life of total righteousness. Since He was a Jew the pathway of obedience required that He obey every detail of the law. Of course He had no choice; He was a baby. But God gave Him parents who were willing to obey the law at every point.

2. **Jesus was given a name that highlights His work** (2:21b). He was called 'Jesus'. The name is a form of the Old Testament name Jehoshua; it means 'the Lord saves'. God had given instructions that this should be His name (1:31). It was God's way of marking out from the very beginning that Jesus was coming to be the Saviour from the guilt and power of sin.

3. **Luke's story goes on to emphasise even more strongly how Jesus kept the law**. According to Leviticus 12:1–4, after giving birth to a son, a woman had to undergo forty days abstention

from worship at the tabernacle. Then she offered a sacrifice for her ceremonial purification. (Luke says 'their' purification; it simply means that Joseph brought the sacrifice for his wife's purification. It is a compressed way of speaking.)

In addition to the purification, the law required that the child be 'presented'. The firstborn son had to be specially offered to God. He was only exempted from working in the temple by being 'redeemed' – by the paying of a sum of money. His mother had to give some silver as a compensation for the fact that he was not going to be left for lifelong service in the temple.

Mary fulfils these requirements of the law (2:22). Luke specially draws attention to the way in which Mary's acts were obeyed the requirements of the law (2:23).

4. **Luke makes clear that Jesus' family were poor**. Mary offers a sacrifice of two pigeons or turtle-doves (2:25). The law required that a one-year old lamb should be offered. But if a family were desperately poor the law had a special provision for them. Turtle-doves or pigeons were easy to catch. The poor could capture them for no charge. Needy people were allowed to offer two doves or pigeons instead of the more expensive lamb. The fact that Joseph and Mary offer the two birds is a proof that they were not rich people. It is a proof that financial prosperity is not absolutely guaranteed to every godly person. Mary was highly honoured in being chosen as Jesus' mother. But her being highly honoured by God did not bring her guaranteed financial prosperity.

5. **Jesus was recognised as the long-awaited awaited Messiah** (2:25–30). There was a righteous and law-abiding man living in Jerusalem who was specially waiting for the coming of the Saviour. He was expecting Him as the 'consolation' of Israel, the One who would bring many spiritual blessings which would comfort Jewish believers after their centuries of defeat by various pagan enemies (2:25). He was obviously a man close to God, and God had let him know that the Saviour would come within his lifetime (2:26).

He is led by the Holy Spirit to come to the temple at the very moment when Jesus is being brought by His parents for the various legal ceremonies that have to be carried out (2:27).

He takes the child and give a prophecy while the child is in his arms (2:28).

He knows he has been allowed to live long enough to see the era of salvation which is about to begin (2:29–30).

He rejoices in the fact that such salvation is to be for the whole world. It is *'for all people'* (2:31), a light for revealing things to Gentiles (2:32). It is notable that Luke has been stressing how law-abiding Jesus and His parents were. Yet though Jesus was born as a Jew 'under the law', yet His salvation is not only for Jews. The Jewish Saviour is Saviour of the world.

Joseph and Mary are amazed at Simeon's words (2:33). He is a man of the Holy Spirit. When Jesus comes into the world, there is a burst of the Holy Spirit's inspiration. Godly men and women sing His praise as He comes into the world.

Simeon continues. Many will 'fall' because of Jesus. Others will 'rise' because of Him (2:34). He will face much opposition (2:34b). Mary herself will suffer greatly (2:35). The secret thoughts and purposes of many people will be brought out and disclosed (2:35b).

When Jesus comes people react in one way or another. No one can be neutral or impartial. Some will fall. They will reject Jesus in anger and disbelief. Others will rise. They will find in Jesus One who brings forgiveness, the knowledge of God and the power of the Holy Spirit. In one way or another the true thoughts of the heart get exposed when Jesus draws near. Some reveal their faith; others reveal their unbelief and antagonism. But no one stays the same, when Jesus comes.

Chapter 12

A Ministry of Prophecy

(Luke 2:36–40)

After Simeon comes Anna. The elderly man is followed by the elderly woman.

1. **We have here an example of a special ministry given to an elderly widow**. Anna is a prophetess. She had been married for seven years but then had lost her husband. At the time of our story she had been a widow 'up to eighty-four years' (not 'for' eighty-four years). This seems to mean that she is eighty-four years old at the time of her speaking about Jesus (2:36). Although her home area was Asher in the far north, she had come to Jerusalem and lived in the temple area. She spent her time in praying and giving words of prophecy to those who came to the temple (2:37).

An eighty-four-year-old widow might seem to be a person who will not have much of a ministry among the people of God. But God has a ministry for every one of His people. Every believer has something to do for God. Anna was called to spend much of her time in prayer. As she prays, God gives her words of prophecy to share with those who come to the temple.

2. **Anna's ministry at this point consisted of confirming someone else's ministry**. We are not told exactly what Anna said. She publicly praised God for sending Jesus but we are not told exactly what words she used (2:38). The more important matter was that she confirmed what Simeon had just said. Two godly people had been brought to the temple at the very point where Jesus was being brought for the necessary legal ceremonies.

3. **Anna's ministry arose out of great prayerfulness**. These two people, Simeon and Anna, were bringing messages from

God that would sustain Mary in years to come. When Mary first heard about Jesus she rejoiced (see 1:46–47), but there are years of great suffering ahead of her. She will witness the rejection of her Son. She will see Him hang upon a cross. There will be times when she will wonder whether everything she thought she knew was actually wrong. She needs special encouragement to be able to keep going for many years.

God's timing will encourage her. She will always remember that at the very point when she was bringing Jesus to the temple, two godly people were led by the Holy Spirit to arrive at that very moment to bring her words of encouragement from God. She will have to hold on the fact that an angel visited her (see 1:26–38). She will remember that her son was conceived without any human father. She could never be mistaken about that! She will remember that two of the most godly people in Jerusalem gave her special words of encouragement at the time of Jesus fulfilling the law of Moses. Then she will recall that she was warned that a sword would pierce her heart. The way of the Saviour would be a way of suffering for Him and for her.

The suffering would not go on forever. One day Mary would be present on the Day of Pentecost. She would see what was involved in her Son being the Saviour of the world. She would know that He was risen from the dead, and was appointed by the Father to be the King of the universe.

Prophecy arises out of great prayerfulness. Anna is called a prophetess, yet we are not told much about her prophecy; we are told more about her prayerfulness. God reveals secrets to us as we pray.

Prophecy is intended to encourage. Anna's word following after Simeon's words would give Mary encouragement for many years.

3. **Anna's ministry consisted of spreading good news to individuals**. She was not a preacher. She simply spoke about Jesus to everyone she knew who was waiting for God's Saviour. There were people in Jerusalem who were expecting a day of salvation, and a day when Jerusalem would be delivered from pagan enemies. They were expecting a Saviour to come, many to be saved, and Jerusalem to be given its

freedom (in that order!) Anna knew that her task was to tell everyone God's programme had started moving forward. The Saviour had been born!

These are the marks of prophetic ministry. It arises from great prayerfulness. Such a ministry may well come to someone whose freedom in life is restricted, a widow, a person who has suffered greatly or is in a lonely position. It is a ministry that encourages, and it does so by pointing people to Jesus and His salvation.

After their visit to Jerusalem to fulfil the law, Joseph and Mary returned to Nazareth in Galilee (2:39). The Saviour was born. He now had to grow up. He would not start His main ministry until He was a man. But He was a real human being. The Saviour was not an angel or a spirit. He was a human being. He knew then, and He knows now, exactly what it is to live a real human life. He grew physically. *'The child grew up and was strong'* (2:40). Jesus was a real human being. He followed the normal processes of eating and sleeping, getting exercise, taking care of His health. He grew up physically.

He grew in wisdom. He knew God from His earliest days. At some point He came to know that He was God's Son in a unique way. God was the only Father He had.

He even grew spiritually. God's grace and favour were upon Him. He obeyed God in everything. He learned to pray. God was putting Him through the ordinary processes of human life, so that He could be a real human being, able to sympathise with us at every point of our lives.

Chapter 13

Jesus As a Boy

(Luke 2:41–52)

Luke's story takes another step forward, this time over a gap of twelve years. Joseph is still alive. Jesus' mother, Mary, is twelve years older. Jesus has brothers and sisters. Every year the family went to the festival of the Passover. It is perhaps about the year AD 9 when a memorable incident takes place. Jesus is twelve years old.

1. **It is obvious that Jesus as a twelve-year old boy Jesus was trustworthy and capable**. In one particular year, perhaps about AD 8 or 9, Joseph and Mary make their annual journey to Jerusalem for Passover time (2:41–42). They leave Jesus to look after Himself. Then when the festival is over they begin to travel home. They do not make any special efforts to look for Jesus, and so Jesus gets left behind without their realising it (2:43). It may seem rather strange that Joseph and Mary should not at first make any effort to look for Jesus. There can only be one reason for it. They are very used to the fact that Jesus is utterly trustworthy and is quite capable of looking after Himself. He had a good relationship with relatives and friends, so it was quite possible that He was travelling with them. Joseph and Mary have no anxiety whatsoever about the fact that they have not seen their twelve-year old son.

This can only mean that in days gone by Jesus has happily mixed with other members of the family and has been quite capable of looking after Himself. The parents are so used to Jesus' doing this that they make no arrangements for Jesus to travel back with them and for a day they do not even worry about His absence. They are quite sure He has made His own arrangements. The story gives us a glimpse of the boy Jesus. It is obvious that He was utterly trustworthy. One could leave Him to take care of matters and He would be totally responsible in what He did. In the thinking of His parents, Jesus needed no special care. He had proved many times that He was capable of caring for Himself.

2. **Jesus as a young boy was evidently a very independent person**. He was a young man who 'did His own thing' and often made His own arrangement for His life, even when He was twelve years old. In those days when Jesus had been at the Passover festival, He was doing a lot of thinking for Himself. He was only a boy but He knew much about the faith of Israel and He had thought much about Himself. He knew that God was His Father in a very special way. Anyone who wishes to go far with God will have to learn to think and act for himself or herself.

3. **Jesus as a young boy was zealous to discover everything He could about God and His will**. Although Jesus was the Son of God, He was also a genuine man. He did not know everything all in one instant. He had to learn and grow. So He took every opportunity to learn more of the things of God. Jesus' parents eventually discover that Jesus is missing (2:44) and they return to look for Him (2:45). After three days they find Him. He is quite happy and untroubled. He has been staying overnight near to the temple. He is spending every moment He can listening to anyone who might be able to help Him understand the Scriptures. He asks them questions, discussing every aspect of the things of God (2:46). Everyone who hears Him is amazed at His wisdom (2:47). He was taking it upon Himself to learn as much as He could from those who might know the Old Testament Scriptures. We have to learn to grow in the things of God. Even the Son of God, Jesus Himself, had to grow. Even He did not know everything all in one instant. He was an authentic human being, and men and women do not learn everything in one flash.

4. **Despite His very great position in the kingdom of God Jesus was willing to submit to authority**. His parents return. They feel that Jesus has treated them badly (2:48). Actually the problem is not with Jesus. The problem is with them.

Mary and Joseph were told years ago that Jesus was unique. They must expect Him to be active in the things of God. He is now twelve years old and in Jewish culture a twelve-year-old boy has passed into a new stage of maturity and can be expected to show greater responsibility. They should have taken it for granted that Jesus would be wanting to move forward in His understanding of the things of God and would take advantage of a Passover festival. Twenty-five years later He would be crucified at a Passover festival, and He would Himself be the Passover Lamb of God! They should have known that He would be at the temple (2:49).

Jesus submits to them. He knows more than His parents. They did not quite understand Him (2:50). He has greater spiritual wisdom, yet He submits to them. Although He is the Son of God He does not ask them to obey Him; He obeys them. Mary just keeps thoughtfully considering what has happened (2:51).

5. **Jesus grew into readiness for the purpose of God**. Because the Son of God was a real human being, He developed steadily until He was ready for the greatest purpose of God in His life.

(i) He grew mentally. *'Jesus increased in wisdom'*.

(ii) He grew physically. *'Jesus increased ... in stature'*.

(iii) He grew spiritually. *'Jesus increased ... in favour with God'*.

(iv) He grew socially. *'Jesus increased ... in favour with ... man'*.

There was a steady all-round development in Jesus' life. God was getting Him ready.

Chapter 14

History and the Holy Spirit

(Luke 3:1–3)

Each of the four gospels begins with some kind of title or introduction (Mark 1:1; Matthew 1:1; Luke 1:1–4; John 1:1–18). Then two of the gospels tell stories from Jesus' youth (Matthew 1:2–2:23; Luke 1:5–2:52).

At the next stage, all four gospels tell us something of the events at the beginning of Jesus' ministry. We start a section of Jesus' story which runs from about mid AD 29 to Passover AD 30.

John the Baptist has started ministering. Somewhere between mid AD 29 and Passover AD 30 John baptised Jesus (Mark 1:2–11; Matthew 3:1–17; Luke 3:1–18, 21–22; John 1:19–34). Then Jesus was tempted (Mark 1:12–13; Matthew 4:1–11; Luke 4:1–13). John's Gospel lets us know that at about this time Jesus first met some of His disciples and spent time with them (John 1:35–52). He visited Cana (John 2:1–11) and Capernaum (John 2:12). Then in AD 30 He returned to Jerusalem for the first Passover of His ministry (John 2:13). He cleansed the temple (2:14–22), did many signs (2:23–25), counselled Nicodemas (3:1–21) and for several months (perhaps April–December AD 30) ministered in Judea. The ministries of Jesus and John the Baptist were both going on at the same time (John 3:22–36). Then there came a time where it was dangerous for Jesus in Judea (John 4:1–4). John the Baptist was imprisoned and Jesus went to Galilee (Mark 1:14–15; Mathew 4:12; Luke 4:14). On the way he ministered in Samaria (John 4:5–45). Our interest is in the way in which Luke tells the story.

1. **We notice again Luke's special interest in history**. Luke 3:1–2 finds six ways of pin-pointing exactly when it was that the ministry of Jesus began. We are told which Roman emperor was ruling, which Roman governor was working in Judea, which members of the Herod family were reigning over three areas of Israel (Galilee; Iturea and Trachonitis; Abilene), and which high priests were reigning over the Jerusalem religious scene. Luke is interested in dates and rulers. He gives a historical framework for his story.

The Christian must be interested in history if he is to be faithful to his Bible. Luke also has a great interest in the Holy Spirit. There are more references to the Holy Spirit in Luke's Gospel than in Matthew and Mark. It is Luke who has a second volume which tells of the day of Pentecost and of what happened as a result.

These two emphases – history and the Holy Spirit – are equally important. Some people are only interested in the facts of the Christian faith. They look at the gospel simply as a matter of events that happened a long time ago that we believe in. Others are interested in the Holy Spirit. 'It does not matter what happened in history,' they say. 'It only matters what happens by the Holy Spirit.'

Actually both history and the Holy Spirit are equally important in our way of looking at the gospel. One of the differences between the Christian faith and the world's religions is that we believe in certain crucial events which happened in history. Jesus received the Holy Spirit when He was baptised by John; it is a fact of history. Jesus died. Jesus rose from the dead. Jesus poured out the Holy Spirit and created the Spirit-powered Church. These are all events of history. When we believe them and receive them, they become facts in our hearts as well. The Holy Spirit makes Jesus real to us **now**. But the history is first. These events happen in world-history, so that they are out in the open for anyone to see. Luke writes a history book about what happened.

2. **God acted to restore His work**. For hundreds of years there has been no great prophet. Suddenly God takes hold of a person and communicates a message to him. *'The word of God came to John ... in the wilderness'* (3:2).

He was the son of Zacharias, a godly priest. God gives us the right background. Sometimes God takes hold of a person whose background is entirely pagan, and uses him. Yet it is also true that sometimes spiritual parents contribute to what we later do for God. John was prepared by God to have a unique ministry. His upbringing was part of his preparation.

At this point in the story, he had been a believer for many years. We know that he was full of the Holy Spirit (1:15). He had grown up as a believing young man.

He was a man who lived with unusual self-restraint. He had been led by God to live in a lonely spot, in the wilderness of Judea (3:2).

He was a preacher. Spiritual restoration takes place when God raises up a preacher who will preach about sin and judgement, about salvation and the grace of God.

Here was a man who brought into being a new people ready to do God's will. It is not enough to preach. When the Church is being restored, there has to be another step. The preacher has to gather people together and get a community of people who will represent God in His world. John not only preaches; he also baptises people.

What was John's baptism? It was immersion into water. The water did not do anything. It was spiritual symbolism. The water symbolised the cleansing of sins. Getting oneself baptised expressed the fact that you were believing in John's message. It was an expression of repentance. It was a way of publicly saying 'I have changed my mind about my life. I have come to see that I must believe in the promises of God and I am trusting in what I have heard in the preaching of this man, John the Baptist.'

Because baptism was a public and visible sign it created a community, a people who been baptised by John.

When God restores His Church He sends a preacher and He enlarges His church with a new company of believers.

Chapter 15

Revival Preaching

(Luke 3:4–9)

The gospels refer to the way in which John's ministry fulfilled Scripture (Mark 1:2–3; Luke 3:4–6; Matthew 3:3). All of them quote Isaiah 40:3; Mark also quotes Malachi 3:1 and Luke adds Isaiah 40:4–5 (in Luke 3:5–6).

1. **John was exercising a ministry of restoration** (3:4–6). He did his work by preaching. He was *'the voice ... crying in the wilderness ... '* (3:4). It was a lonely work. The spiritual leaders in Israel had wandered far from God's truth. Israel was in a period of spiritual decay and deadness. Their spiritual leaders were in the work of God simply for their own advantage. Preaching had almost died out. Godly people were hard to find.

But God does not let His Church die out. From time to time He sends spiritual revival to His people. 'Revival' is not something that we organise; it is something that God does. No one was 'organising' a revival in the days of John the Baptist. God was simply raising up a man to bring many of His people to their senses.

God does not call unsaved people to 'prepare' for salvation. Believe on the Lord Jesus Christ and you will be saved! But John is preaching to Israel, to the common people. Many of them have faith in the promises of God but they have become cold and backslidden. When God's people wish to be restored to newness of life, they need to take action to get their lives right. They need to make a straight road for Him (3:4). If they would do that, impossible obstacles would be cleared out of the way. The valleys and mountains that make travel so complicated would be flattened so that the pathway would be easier (3:5). The crooked and the rough would be rectified (3:5).

Also there would be a result in the lives of others. *'All flesh shall see the salvation of our God'* (3:6). The entire human race would get to experience the salvation that was coming to Israel (3:6), if His people would get ready for what God was about to do.

2. **John was exercising a ministry of warning** (3:7–9). God was drawing near to Israel and was offering His people a way to return to Him.

John the Baptist took note of people who were joining the crowds but had no real interest in having their lives changed. They were like snakes wriggling away from a fire in the countryside (3:7). They had no interest in living a godly life; they simply wanted to escape from God's judgement. They thought that they were good Jews because they were descended from Abraham. They imagined that they would be safe if they became a bit religious and joined John the Baptist's meetings (3:8a). But John warns them. God does not require a good ancestry. He can raise children to himself from the dead stones (3:8b). Salvation does not require a starting point in Jewish ancestry (or Christian ancestry!) God starts from zero when He brings us to salvation (3:8b).

These 'religious' people are still under the judgement of God. Unless they come to experience salvation they will still soon be punished for their sins. God's punishment of sin will be like chopping down a fruitless tree and throwing it into the fire.

Fire is often used as a picture of judgement; Luke's references to fire are in 3:9, 16, 17; 9:54; 12:49; 17:29; 22:55. Fire exterminates, wipes out of existence. Rubbish is thrown into fire (Luke 3:9). The fire cannot be put out; it is 'unquenchable' (Luke 3:17). It exterminates rubbish. So it 'cleanses' (3:17) by wiping out of existence the dirt (3:17); it 'burns up'. Every reference to 'burning up'[1] in the New Testament (Matthew 3:12; 13:30, 40; Luke 3:17; Acts 19:19; 1 Corinthians 3:15; Hebrews 13:11; 2 Peter 3:10; Revelation 8:7; 17:16; 18:8) has the idea of utter extermination. What is burned up 'passes away' (2 Peter 3:10). John warned that everything of the lives of religious people would come under the exterminating fire of God, like rubbish being thrown into a burning pit, unless they find salvation through John's message. (The parable of the rich man and Lazarus makes it clear that the fire of God's judgement continues after death; 'I am in agony in this flame' said the rich man, Luke 16:24.)

3. **John was exercising a ministry of detailed holiness teaching**. Luke 3:10–14 has no parallel in Matthew or Mark. John gave detailed instruction about how the godly life worked out in practice. The essence of the godly life is generosity and kindness (3:10–11). People working for the Romans as tax collectors or soldiers could continue their work but should do so in a just and godly manner. Tax collectors should abandon their oppression (3:12–13). Soldiers could continue their work but should not use their forceful ways to oppress people (3:14). John is not an absolute pacifist; he allows his converts to be soldiers. But he requires that they do their work with righteousness.

It is clear that one part of John's ministry involved detailed teaching in the ways of righteousness. John's revival-movement was a 'holiness movement'. Today the entire Christian Church is to be a 'holiness movement'. Every part of the Bible is 'holiness teaching'. John's ministry is an 'Elijah-ministry', a restoring ministry, a work in which God raises up a man to bring the Church back to what it ought to be. It begins with the preaching of Jesus; 'the Lord' (3:4) who is about to come is Jesus. He is a Saviour who gives new birth; He raises up children for God (3:8). He is a Saviour who leads people into ways of godliness. He is the Saviour who comes for 'all flesh' (3:6). He is the One who one day will be the judge. This is what 'revival preaching' is. It is the message of God's hatred of sin, and God's provision of a Saviour, applied in power to the consciences of men and women.

Note

1. Greek *kataischuno*.

Chapter 16

Preparing the Way for Jesus

(Luke 3:15–22)

People were amazed at John the Baptist's ministry. Many people were expecting a Messiah to come soon; so they wondered whether perhaps John was the one who was to come to rescue them (3:15).

1. **John pointed to Jesus as the One who gives the Spirit**. John deliberately presented himself as an altogether lower person than Jesus. *'I baptise you with water . . . He shall baptise you with the Holy Spirit and with fire . . .'* (3:16). We note that John's water-baptism is **contrasted** with baptism with the Spirit. No water-baptism conveys the Spirit. Water-baptism is an expression of God's promises; and when people get themselves baptised they are expressing repentance (in the case of John's baptism), or faith in Jesus (in the case of Christian baptism). God and man are saying something to each other through this simple ceremony. But the water does not convey the Spirit.

Jesus, says John, has an altogether greater ministry: that of baptising with the Holy Spirit (3:16). Jesus is 'the Stronger One', a person with altogether greater spiritual power than John. John cannot give the Holy Spirit; nor can any other human being. Only Jesus can give the Holy Spirit.

The 'baptism with the Spirit' is what happened on the Day of Pentecost. It is the work of Jesus in which He 'pours out' the Holy Spirit upon a believer (or upon many believers at the same time), and in which there is given assurance of salvation, boldness in witness, ease in prayer, consciousness of God's love, joy unspeakable and an intense awareness of the presence of Jesus in the believer's life.

2. **John pointed to Jesus as the One who is both Saviour and Judge**. *'He shall baptise with the Spirit and with fire'*, said John the Baptist. How are we meant to take the reference to fire? In the light of the surrounding references to the fire of God's judgement, John's phrase seems to mean that the coming Saviour would bring both salvation and (for those who refused salvation) the fire of God's judgement.

John speaks as a prophet. Like many of the prophets of the Old Testament he sees **everything** God will do to bring in God's kingdom. His vision of the future includes Jesus' outpouring of the Spirit and Jesus' outpouring of the fire of God's anger against sin. John has a **total** vision of Jesus as Saviour and Judge. As John's prediction was fulfilled, the salvation was before the judgement. The baptism of the Spirit is before the baptism with fire. This time-gap gave John some problems. A time came when he wondered what had happened to the baptism with fire (see Luke 7:18–23). It was this that made him doubt at one point whether Jesus really was the Messiah. Actually the 'fire' would be later than the Spirit. Jesus would be Saviour first, and return as Judge later. John pointed to one who would be Saviour and Judge (3:17). This was the message he preached with great power (3:18).

3. **John's preaching of holiness brought him into personal suffering**. Luke 3:19–20 is one of a few places in Luke's Gospel where Luke tells a story out of chronological order. Mark and Matthew tell the story at a much later stage of their gospels (see Mark 6:17–29; Matthew 14:3–12), but Luke brings this matter forward because he wants at this point to complete his picture of John the Baptist. He tells the story briefly. Luke's readers would know the story for themselves.

John's preaching was detailed and fearless. He was willing to press upon Herod the need for him to be righteous in his marriage. Herod had wrongly divorced his first wife, the daughter of the Arabian king, Aretas, and he had persuaded his brother's wife to abandon her husband and marry him. John was the leader of a national movement in which many in the land were finding salvation. John was calling for repentance among all people everywhere. He could not leave such a scandalous sin unrebuked. But it brought suffering into

John's life. John was imprisoned. Luke tells the story here to let us see another aspect of John's character and ministry. He was a man who said what had to be said, regardless of what personal suffering it might cause him.

4. **John's preaching would soon give way to Jesus' preaching** (3:21–22). Jesus was on the verge of commencing His ministry but certain things had to come first. First Jesus identified Himself with sinners. He was baptised, not in His case, to express repentance, but to put Himself among sinners who needed repentance.

As He was obedient in this way He was given the Holy Spirit (3:21–22). The Spirit came upon Him as He was praying. Luke likes to stress the work of the Spirit and he likes to emphasise prayer. The two themes are connected. We are likely to receive blessings of the Spirit as we pray. The disciples were in an upper room praying, when the events of the Day of Pentecost started with the outpouring of the Holy Spirit.

Even Jesus needed the baptism with the Holy Spirit. As for us, so for Him the gift of the Spirit was an empowering for ministry and an assurance of sonship. He received an added confirmation of His being God's Son ('You are my beloved Son') and was also addressed as the suffering Servant of the prophecies of Isaiah (the words 'in whom I am well pleased' echo Isaiah 42:1). The Holy Spirit took the appearance of a dove. As a dove brought evidence of a new world at the time of the flood, so the dove-like Holy Spirit comes upon Jesus. The Holy Spirit's power now rests upon the man Jesus and so enable Him to bring into being a new kingdom of grace.

Chapter 17

Jesus' Ancestors

(Luke 3:23–38)

A person's ancestors have a lot to do with his identity. At this point Luke shares with us Jesus' 'genealogy' (list of ancestors). Again one might think that this section is out of chronological order. It could have come at the beginning of the gospel. But Luke has been dealing with the events that prepared the way for Jesus. Now he comes to focus on Jesus Himself. So this is a good point at which to insert the genealogy of Jesus to show who Jesus is and how He fits into world history.

There are some differences between this genealogy and the one in Matthew's Gospel. Luke's genealogy starts from Jesus and works backwards until it reaches Adam, and God (in 3:38). Matthew's genealogy starts with Abraham and moves forward until it gets to Jesus (Matthew 1:2–17).

The genealogy begins with a note of Jesus' approximate age at the time His ministry began (3:23a) and a reminder that Jesus was not really the biological son of Joseph but was only his son legally (3:23b).

The section in 3:23c–31 runs from Jesus back to David. It proves that Jesus is the descendant of David. It is Joseph's ancestors that are being listed. Jesus was the legal son of Joseph. *'He was, in the minds of the people the son of Joseph'*, says 3:23b. Joseph is said to be 'son of Heli, son of Matthat' (3:23–24) but in Matthew 1:15–16 he is the son of 'Jacob', who was the son of 'Matthan'. This could mean that the genealogy is Mary's genealogy and Joseph was treated as Heli's son because of his marriage to Mary. But more likely Matthew's genealogy is a list of those who were entitled to be the king of Israel. It is a succession-list. Luke's list is more a list of the physical descent although there might be some Levirate marriages in it (places where a man begot a son with his brother's wife because the brother had died). Joseph was probably biologically the son of Heli (Luke 3:23) but if Jacob (Matthew 1:16) had no sons Joseph would have inherited the royal line from him. Matthew's list runs through Solomon.

The names in Luke 3:24–27 are different from the names in Matthew 1:13–16. The genealogy is being traced through a different part of the family at this point. There is no problem in this. It often happens that a person can trace his ancestry to a figure of long ago through more than one section of the family. Luke has more names than Matthew. This probably means that Matthew is leaving out some generations. In the genealogies the word 'son' may mean 'descendant'. In Luke 3:27b *'Rhesa'* is an Aramaic word meaning 'prince' and the line should be probably be translated 'son of Prince Zerubbabel'.

In Luke 3:27d Shealtiel is son of Neri, son of Melchi; but in Matthew 1:12 he is son of Jeconiah. Matthew is giving the line of entitlement to the throne of David. Luke's list is more strictly biological.

In Luke 3:27e–31 the names are totally different. Luke's list runs through Nathan. Matthew's list (Matthew 1:5–8) runs through Solomon.

The section in Luke 3:32–34 runs back from David to Abraham. These are more-or-less the same as the names in Matthew 1:2–5. They show that Jesus descended from Abraham.

The section in 3:34–38 runs back from Abraham to Adam. They show that Jesus was not only the one who fulfilled the promises to the House of David, not only the one that fulfilled the promises to Abraham, but also the one who fulfilled God's intention for the entire human race. Matthew is specially interested in Israel; Luke is specially interested in the fact that Jesus comes for the entire human race.

At this stage of Jewish history Jewish people preserved the records of their ancestry. Jewish people sent the names of their children to be officially recorded.[1] Those who were descended from David would be especially careful to keep records because the Old Testament predicted the Messiah would come from the line of David.

There are seventy-five people in this list of Jesus' forefathers. Jesus fulfils the promises of God concerning Himself that were given to David, to Abraham, and to Adam.

1. As **Son of David**, Jesus was the One who was anointed by the Spirit and rules over God's total people. David was given a promise that one day there would come someone who would follow the pattern he had started.

2. As **Son of Abraham**, Jesus fulfils the promise that Abraham's seed will bring world-wide blessing. Abraham was promised that one day he would have a seed through whom Israel would come into being and through whom eventually all the nations of the world would be blessed.

3. As **Son of Adam**, Jesus is genuinely human, and is fully qualified to minister to the human race. To Adam was given the promise that one day what had happened through him would eventually be reversed through a member of the human race who be 'the seed of the woman', but apparently not the seed of Adam!

4. As **Son of God**, Jesus is like Adam who was also 'son of God' (Luke 3:38). The first man was brought into being by a direct act of God. Jesus is a second Adam who re-starts the human race on a new basis.

As Son of David, Jesus is our king. As Son of Abraham, Jesus links us into the world-wide blessing He intends for the human race. As Son of Adam, Jesus is capable of being our sympathiser, for He is a fellow human being. As Son of God, Jesus has the power to protect us and bring us to glory, since He was specially brought into being for this very purpose.

Note

1. See Josephus, *Against Apion*, 1:8.

Chapter 18

Jesus' Temptation

(Luke 4:1–13)

Before Jesus' ministry began, three things happened in His life. He needed to be baptised, to receive the Spirit, and to prove He could withstand temptation. Luke's next section (4:1–13) shows that Jesus could resist temptation.

Every Christian who wishes to be used by God has to overcome temptation. In the life of any Christian there will come a time when God lets a time of testing come upon us. The same thing happened to Jesus early in His lifetime. He was quite young, in His early thirties. He had three years of intense ministry before Him when He would minister to thousands of people. But He needed to be tested first.

1. **Jesus' experience of being tested came immediately after His receiving the power of the Holy Spirit**. Luke emphasises the result of Jesus' being baptised with the Spirit. The Holy Spirit was powerfully working in Jesus' life, such that He was 'full' of the Spirit (4:1) and was strongly conscious of the Spirit's direct guidance. He knew that He was being led by the Holy Spirit to spend a period of just under six weeks in fasting. He needed to specially give Himself to seeking God's will, God's power, and God's guidance as His new ministry was about to begin. The greatest blessings might well be followed by the greatest attacks from Satan.

2. **Three temptations were pressed upon Jesus**. Jesus was tempted by the devil for the whole of the period of forty days, but three particular temptations came at the end of His weeks of fasting at a time when He was exceptionally hungry (4:2).

There was the temptation to put His material welfare above the will of God (4:3–4). Jesus did not perform miracles for His own benefit and it certainly was not God's will that the hunger He was experiencing after much fasting should be miraculously ended by the creation of bread! Jesus was learning, right at the beginning of His work, that God would not want Him to perform miracles for His own advantage. No one will be much used by God unless he or she learns to abandon 'ministry' purely for the sake of one's own advantage.

There was the temptation to get to a position of authority and glory by the worship of Satan (4:5–8). Jesus needed authority and it was God's will that He should get 'glory', but both His authority and His glory were to come from God alone.

There was also the temptation to prove His Messiahship in a sensational manner (4:9–12). Psalm 91 was often thought by the rabbis – the Jewish teachers – to be about the Messiah. There was also a traditional belief that the Messiah would show Himself by standing on the roof of the temple.[1] So Satan invited Jesus to stand on the highest part of the temple which stood out conspicuously so that everyone could see it. He suggested that if Jesus leapt from the temple and expected God to save Him, everyone would know that He was the expected Saviour. It might seem an odd thing to do; but Satan often prompts people to do odd things! He backed up what he had to say with a word from the Scriptures! *'It is written, "He shall give his angels charge over you . . ." '* says the devil (4:10, quoting Psalm 91). The devil knows how to use the Bible and can twist it to his own advantage when he wants to!

3. **Jesus was able to withstand temptation**. He defeated Satan partly by His prayerfulness. He had just been praying. He was full of confidence in God. It is important to realise that this spiritual preparedness which we find in Jesus was the result of the way in which He has been living **before** special temptations came upon Him. Strength in temptation depends partly on what spiritual state we are in at the time of the temptation. The degree to which something tempts us depends much upon us.

Because of His submission to God's written word, Jesus was able to resist temptation. He had a clear mind and a firm will because of His dependence on God's written word. Jesus did not have to hold a long discussion with Satan. Nor did He spend a lot of time wondering whether maybe the devil's suggestions were good ideas. He was in a lifelong habit of instant obedience to the will of God revealed in the Old Testament. 'It is written . . . ' was His instant answer to Satan. He knows the answer to these temptations instantly. His life depends not upon bread but upon God (4:4; see Deuteronomy 8:3). No one can demand His worship except God (4:8; see 6:3). Foolish and sensational methods of getting attention would be disobedience to God's will and so would be 'testing God'. To 'test God' is to act out of the will of God and so is a kind of 'test' since it almost invites God to act in rebuke and chastisement. The Old Testament said *'You shall not test the Lord your God'* (4:12; see Deuteronomy 6:16). All three of Jesus' replies to Satan are taken from the book of Deuteronomy. It was presumably the book on which He had been meditating during His forty days in the wilderness.

When Jesus resisted the devil in this way, the devil left him. Satan left 'for a time' (4:13). He would tempt Jesus again many times but for the moment he gave up. When we withstand temptation the devil will leave us for a while. God knows how to give us breaks from the devil's attacks. We are not attacked all the time. When Satan seeks to ruin us our ability to stand depends much on our **past** prayerfulness, and our commitment to God's written word.

Note

1. See the Midrash known as *Pesiqta Rabbati*, 162a.

Chapter 19

A Prophet in His Own Country

(Luke 4:14–30)

Luke passes over the early ministry of Jesus in Judea which is recorded in John 1:35–3:36 and which probably took place in about April to December, AD 30. In early AD 31 Jesus left Judea and travelled to Galilee. From John's Gospel we hear of some of the events on the journey (John 4:1–46a) and of the second miracle in Galilee (John 4:46b–54). Galilee will be Jesus' home base. The power of the Spirit rests on Him (4:14a). He soon becomes well-known (4:14b). His preaching was well received (4:15). Luke 4:16–30 brings forward an incident which Mark records as taking place later. Luke 4:23 shows that this story is not the first event in Jesus' Galilean ministry.

Jesus visited His home town in Nazareth (4:16). He went there 'as His custom was' (4:16), and He was invited to expound a passage of Scripture. Jesus read a passage from Isaiah (4:17) and applied it to Himself (4:18–21). At first the people were impressed (4:22). Yet Jesus went on to say that they were not really heeding what He was saying. They simply wanted Him to do some more miracles as they had heard He had done elsewhere (4:23). Their familiarity with Him was preventing them from really taking Him seriously (4:24).

1. **There is a danger of a superficial approach to Jesus which does not allow His Word to reach our hearts**. People like religion. These people in Nazareth are in a synagogue! Religious people want God to help them materially, to watch over their health, to make life pleasant for them.

But have they really understood Jesus? He is claiming that He Himself is uniquely empowered by the Spirit. He comes to fulfil the Scripture. The Old Testament is about Him. He has a message which will transform the lives of the poor, if they will heed it. It will heal broken hearts. It will release people from various kinds of bondage. It will open blind eyes. Jesus' ministry in Israel is in fact a 'day of Jubilee'. Luke 4:19 is echoing the language of the 'Jubilee year' in the Old Testament.

Yet what they really want is to see some miracles. *'What we have heard done in Capernaum, do also here!'*

2. **They do not respond to what God really wants to do in their lives**. The message is greater than they realise. A prophet is not welcome in his own town. Jesus' own people were not receiving Him. Sometimes God sends His gospel to those who have been total strangers to Him in the past. Gentiles received God's blessings more than Israelites in the days of Elijah (4:25–26) and Elisha (4:27). Jesus is not just a son of Nazareth; He is God's Saviour for the entire world including the Gentiles!

Jesus' ministry is a 'Jubilee occasion'. He will transform individuals and He will transform society. He will forgive sins. He will abolish everything that holds back human liberty and joy and progress. He will provide food, shelter, clothes. The year of Jubilee! It is no wonder the people think this is marvellous preaching.

People like messages about society being changed and liberty introduced. Yet we do not always appreciate the way in which God works. Jesus changes society by changing people! These people of Nazareth are about to attempt to murder Jesus! 'Society' will not be changed unless people like them are changed! Jesus is preaching 'good news' to them. He is offering them spiritual release. Their blindness is spiritual. Their need is not purely social. The miracles Jesus performs are simply signs of Jesus' power and authenticity. These people from Nazareth need release from prison as much as anyone. They are experiencing oppression not just from the Romans but from the power of sin in their own lives. The 'Jubilee' year in Israel provided for the restoration of freedom to all impoverished Israelites (see Leviticus 25:28). If he was a slave, his slavery came to an end. If he had lost land, he got his land back.

Jesus stops mid-sentence. Isaiah 61:1–2 spoke of 'the Lord's favour' and 'the day of vengeance of our God'. But Jesus stopped in the middle of a sentence, and quite deliberately 'closed the book'! The prophecy of Isaiah included both salvation and judgement. Jesus was making an announcement. The day of salvation has arrived but the day of judgement has not!

Not all wrongs in society were **immediately** going to be put right. Personal salvation comes before justice chronologically. People have to be right at heart before society will be greatly changed. And they would have to welcome Gentiles in this coming kingdom of Jesus!

It was that point that they did not like. Receiving Gentiles? Never! They wanted miracles. 'Do what you did in Capernaum!' Jesus was offering a salvation that begins with new life coming to individuals, a salvation that would one day reach out and embrace Gentiles.

3. **No one understands God's grace unless it is realised that it is on offer for everyone**. Strangers to grace are more likely to receive it than those who think they know God's grace already. God was merciful to the woman of Zarephath, of all places (4:25–26)! Elijah worked a miracle for a Syrian, and Jesus was likely to do something similar (4:27).

4. **The people reveal that their religion had not really touched their hearts**. This kind of talk makes the people furious with rage (4:28). These respectable synagogue-attendees want to murder Jesus (4:29) by pushing Him over a cliff about three kilometres south-east of Nazareth. But Jesus passes through their midst and no one stops Him (4:30). His escape was itself a little miracle! Their supposed admiration of Jesus has not changed their hearts. They wanted a few miracles and they would like to see the Romans removed from their land. But God wanted to begin with them. While they had murder in their hearts, they were not ready for God's day of Jubilee.

Chapter 20

His Message Was With Authority

(Luke 4:31–44)

Luke now comes to describe the highlights of the Galilean ministry of Jesus. The first phase (Mark 1:14–3:6; Luke 4:14–6:11) perhaps took place during about March AD 31 to about mid-year AD 31. Luke is now following Mark's Gospel quite closely. Luke 4:31–44 is similar to what we have in Mark 1:21–39.

The outstanding characteristic of Jesus is His authority. In the spiritual realm, Jesus only has to speak and things happen. People marvel at the authority of His **teaching** (4:31–32). Then they marvel at the authority He has over **the realm of evil spirits** (4:33–36). When Jesus is in a synagogue a man shows himself to be demonised. The evil spirit recognises and submits to Jesus. As a result Jesus became well known for His spiritual power (4:37).

Then Jesus comes into Simon Peter's house (4:38–39) and reveals that He has authority over **sickness**; He heals Peter's mother-in-law. Many people come in the evening to see Him and He ministers to all of them (4:40–41).

The next day Jesus rises early to pray (4:42–43). This is the source of His authority. When everyone is seeking Him, He is seeking His Father. Soon He leaves Capernaum to preach more widely in the land of the Jewish people (4:44).

1. **In Jesus' story we notice the vital importance of authority**. In some circles 'authority' is not popular. It reminds some people too much of harshness, restraint, bondage, intimidation. In other places 'authority' is very popular. It all depends on which part of the world you are living in and what churches you are familiar with.

Perhaps the first thing that needs to be said is that there is a difference between authority and authoritarianism. True authority does not have to be heavy-handed or tyrannical. True authority is simple. Jesus' authority was simply the fact that He knew what was right with one hundred per cent certainty. When He was preaching and teaching He spoke without harshness or any bullying manner **but He knew that what He said was true**. He knew God would eventually vindicate Him as one who was speaking the truth. This kind of authority is simply a matter of truth held with a clear conscience.

Jesus' authority also involved the fact that **the spiritual world took notice of Him**. When He spoke to demons, they obeyed. When He spoke to a sickness, the sickness obeyed also! He could order a demon to leave. In the same way He could order a sickness to leave. His authority consisted in the fact that spiritual powers recognized Him as a man whom God would want to be honoured.

The fact is that we all need to be under some kind of authority. It does not have to be harsh. We may think we want to be 'free'. That is fine, but our 'freedom' has to be **guided** freedom. It has to be unimpeded movement **along the right lines**. True authority is the kind that Jesus had: loving tender assurance that He was in the will of God.

2. **In Jesus' story we see what it is that produces authority**. Many people want authority: parents, husbands, school-teachers, policemen, politicians, preachers, apostles. Jesus had amazing authority over every realm. His authority was recognized by people. Everyone who had any kind of sickness in Capernaum came seeking Jesus (4:40). Multitudes were searching for Him (4:42). There are two words used here that are found in Luke's Gospel but not in Mark's similar account: they are the words 'preach good news' (different from 'preach' in 4:44 and Mark 1:38) and 'kingdom' (4:43).

What gives a person authority is a message of 'good news'. Many religious ideas are not good news but bad news. It is bad news to tell me that I must somehow find the strength to amend my life. It is bad news to tell me that I have got to be highly religious and have got to go to lots of meetings and do lots of fasting. It is bad news to tell me that I have got to be very clever and understand a lot of doctrinal teaching.

Often the gospel is preached in such a way that it becomes bad news. But the gospel is 'good news' and it is particularly the 'good news about the kingdom'. It is the news that God is willing to act powerfully as a king in my life and in my circumstances. This is why 'multitudes' were looking for Jesus. They had the idea – and they were right – that Jesus was not telling them about laws or rules or religions or intellectual feats of understanding. They had the idea – and they were right – that what He had to say and what He would do would be altogether good news. It is not surprising that Jesus had authority not only over spirits and over sickness; He had authority among the people as well. They kept on coming. They longed to see Him, to hear Him, to have Him work into their lives. That is 'authority' indeed!

3. **In Jesus' story we see the source of Jesus' authority**. Jesus' authority came from God. It was sustained by the fact that He liked to spend time with God. On this occasion He found the opportunity to get away from the people and pray (4:42). Although they were seeking him (4:43), He was not seeking any greater popularity. He was living for God. He knew that He had more work to do in 'the land of the Jews'.[1] His prayerfulness and His commitment to God's will were the source of His authority.

Notes

1. The word 'Judea' in 4:44 does not mean the southern province of Judea but 'the land of the Jews'. Luke simply means Jesus had to go to other towns where Jews were living in addition to Capernaum.

Chapter 21

The Fisherman

(Luke 5:1–11)

Luke 5:1–11 has a story which is not in the other gospels. Luke 4:31–44 is very similar to Mark 1:21–39, and Luke 5:12–6:11 follows Mark 1:40–3:6. But the story in Luke 5:1–11 is found only in Luke's Gospel.

Jesus had already met Peter and some of the other disciples. Shortly after the time of Jesus' being baptised He had met Simon and had given him the name Cephas or Peter (John 1:35–40). Now it is several months later and Jesus has come to preach in Bethsaida where Peter, one of His potential workers, has a fishing business. It is a village on the shores of Lake Galilee. Mark tells the story of Jesus' calling them to ministry (Mark 1:16–20). Luke does not use that story but he inserts this one in Luke 5:1–11 as an equivalent. It must have taken place at about the same time.

1. **Peter sees a display of Jesus' lordship**. Jesus was preaching by the shores of Lake Galilee (5:1). Some fisherman were nearby (5:2). The crowd was pressing upon Jesus so He borrowed Peter's boat, put out to sea a little way, and used the boat as a platform on which to stand as He was preaching (5:3). After the preaching had finished Jesus suggested that Peter should take the boat further out into deeper waters and try catching some fish (5:4). Peter was sceptical (5:5) but he did what Jesus said and the result was that he caught an overwhelmingly large catch of fish (5:6–7).

It was a many-sided lesson for Peter. It showed Peter that Jesus was not only a man with a message from God (5:1); He was also a man whose word was followed by signs of power. It also showed Peter that great and abundant blessing would come if he simply followed Jesus' instructions. Jesus lordship was not just in the realm of spiritual teaching. He was the Lord of fish as well as Lord in the spiritual realm. Every part of God's creation obeys the Lord's commands and achieves His will.

2. **Peter is made to feel his own great sinfulness**. Peter's experience of Jesus' amazing power brings him face to face with the supernatural. He reacts in the way in which we all react when we are suddenly faced with the reality of God. He immediately thinks of his sinfulness.

We all feel this way when suddenly God does something that forces us to realise that He is alive, that He is near at hand, and that He is likely to take action in our lives. A sense of God's presence creates fear and a consciousness of our wickedness. It makes things come back to our minds that we thought we had forgotten. So great can be the sense of our own sinfulness that our first reaction is to feel that it is quite impossible that we could ever be used by God. Surely, we feel, God must punish us. He cannot possibly bless us. It is this kind of feeling that makes Peter say *'Depart from me ... I am a sinful man'* (5:8). Peter feels too sinful to be able to serve God.

3. **Peter experiences God's call despite his own unworthiness**. One might think that Jesus would reply to Peter, 'Yes you are indeed a sinful man ... '. But not one word of rebuke comes from Jesus' lips. When we confess our sinfulness, Jesus does not hold it against us. Peter is harder on himself than Jesus is. The others who were with Peter felt the same way, including James and John (5:9–10a). But the only thing that Jesus says is 'Do not be afraid ... '. Many, many times in the Bible the people of God are told not to be afraid. The angel said the same thing to Zacharias (1:13) and to Mary (1:30). Jesus would tell the disciples *'Fear not, little flock ... '* (12:32). Our sense of sinfulness, our repeated failure, and the sense of how far we have yet to go in the pathway of godliness, all contribute to make our sense of sinfulness oppressive at times. When in some way we are confronted with God we feel almost like despairing. But God does not feel the same way. When we are ready to condemn ourselves, He is far from wishing to condemn us. 'Don't be afraid ... ', He says.

Not only is Jesus not about to reject Peter, He actually still wants Peter for active work in His kingdom.

4. **Peter's future ministry is defined as a new kind of fishing**. *'From now on you shall catch people'*, says Jesus (5:10). There is a sense in which Peter's old job and Peter's new work in the kingdom of Jesus are very similar. He has been a fisherman before; he will be a fisherman again, of people. All Christian ministry starts with bringing newcomers to the salvation that God offers us. The fisherman's great concern is to catch fish. What is the use of being a fisherman if you never catch fish? The more the better. Something similar is true in the work of God. Christian ministry has to start with bringing people into the kingdom of God. There is no Christian church without Christian people. The numbers in the Church of God have to be retained and expanded. It only takes a few years not bothering with outreach and any section of the Church which is careless in that way will find itself severely deteriorated. 'Catching people' is at the heart of the work of the Church of Jesus Christ. Peter is soon to be an apostle. He will be the preacher on the Day of Pentecost. He will be the founder of churches. He will write pages of the Bible – 1 and 2 Peter.

But the heart and centre of his work is fishing for people. The world is the sea. The gospel is the net. Christians are fisherfolk!

Chapter 22

Cleansing and Healing

(Luke 5:12–26)

Luke once again follows material in Mark's Gospel. Luke 5:12–6:11 is very similar to Mark 1:40–3:6. In our passage a leper is cleansed (5:12–26; see Mark 1:40–45), and a paralytic is healed (5:17–26; see Mark 2:1–12).

In looking at miracle-stories one should keep in mind the way in which miracles should be handled by the preacher and expositor. The miracles help us in at least four ways.

1. **Jesus' miracles are pointers to the authenticity of Jesus' ministry**. Here are impossible problems. A man is full of leprosy but knows that if Jesus is willing to act, the leprosy can be cleansed (5:12–13). Although Jesus tells the man to be quiet about what has happened and simply register the fact of his healing with the authorities (5:14), nevertheless the news of Jesus' power goes out everywhere (5:15). It makes Him turn to prayer (5:16). The prayerfulness of Jesus is one of Luke's persistent themes (see 3:21, 22 already).

Soon Jesus is famous. The scholars and religious leaders begin to investigate Jesus, at a time when *'the power of the Lord is present to heal'* (5:17). A paralytic is brought to Jesus. The friends of the paralytic are confident that if only they can get him to Jesus the paralytic will be healed. Some houses at this period of history had tiled roofs. The man's friends go up the outside stairs to the roof. They pull up the tiles of the roof, and make a hole. I suppose one of them swings down on a rope and the others then lower down the paralysed man on his thin wooden bed. Inside the house Jesus and the part of the crowd that have been allowed inside are surprised to see a hole appearing in the ceiling. Maybe the owner of the house makes some protests but the friends promise to repair the house afterwards! Soon the paralytic is in front of Jesus (5:18–19).

Jesus knows that the man is concerned about his sinfulness. Jesus addressed himself first to the spiritual problem (*'Your sins are forgiven'*, 5:20). This offends the observers from Jerusalem (5:21) but Jesus then deals with the man's physical problem (5:22–24). The crowd and the visiting Pharisees were not much impressed at the words of forgiveness, but they are highly impressed at the miraculous healing (5:25–26)! A miracle may be a confirmation of spiritual authority. Jesus underlines this point: *'. . . that you may know that the Son of Man has authority on earth to forgive sins'* (5:24). However it is worth noting that the friends of the man had faith in Jesus before they saw the miracle. The miracle was done for them more than for the Pharisees!

2. **Jesus' miracles are samples of what He can do for us**. What Jesus did before He can do again. However one must not go to extremes in this matter. Miracles cannot be switched on at will, and they cannot be 'taken' by faith. No one can take what God is not giving! The leper knew this. He said *'If you will, you can make me clean'* (5:12). Miracles are subject to Jesus' will but they are a sample of what He can do at any time He likes.

3. **Jesus' miracles are parables of what He is able to do at a deeper level**. Again Jesus makes a point of this very fact. The physical healing illustrates the spiritual healing that had already taken place.

Jesus healed the body as an outward confirmation of the healed relationship with God which had already taken place. He said 'Your sins are forgiven' first, and then added an outward confirmation. This means that the miracles of Jesus can be taken as acted parables of what He is willing to do more deeply within our lives. The Pharisees could not exactly observe the forgiveness of sin and they were sceptical about it. But it was not quite so easy to deny that a paralytic was healed.

Jesus heals us at more than one level. There is a leprosy of the spirit as well as a leprosy of the body. There is a paralysis of spirit as well as a paralysis of body. This man was doubly paralysed. He feared that Jesus might not be willing to forgive him. There was a paralysing fear in his heart as well as a paralysis in his body. Jesus can deal with both!

4. **Jesus' miracles are foretastes of the resurrection**. Miracles cannot be 'switched on' at will; they are subject to the sovereignty of God. Sceptics are not likely to see God at work in any way at all. Yet every miracle is a foretaste of the glory that is to come. Not every person is perfectly healed in this life, and some are not healed at all.

Yet every person of faith is on his way to a healing which will be vastly greater than that of the paralytic. Every miracle is a foretaste of what God will do for His people in the resurrection of the body. One day every ailment will be healed with a healing never to be reversed or undone. The body will decay. Even the paralytic died eventually. There was a day in his life when healing did not come. But the greater healing is yet to come. Every little healing is a forerunner of the greater healing to come in the body when every believer is raised from the dead. Every person who belongs to Jesus will be perfectly healed: 'raised' with 'an imperishable body', 'raised in glory ... raised in power', raised with a body which is a perfect vehicle for the Holy Spirit, the image of the glorified Lord Jesus Christ (1 Corinthians 15:42–44, 49). The cleansed leper and the healed paralytic were only given a foretaste of what is coming to every Christian.[1]

Note

1. See further exposition of these stories in *Mark* (Preaching Through the Bible), chs. 3–4.

Chapter 23

New Wine, New Wineskins

(Luke 5:27–39)

Luke is still following Mark's Gospel. In our present passage Levi (also called Matthew) is summoned to be converted and to join Jesus' ministry-team (5:27–32; see Mark 2:13–17), and a conversation takes place about fasting and about 'new wine and new wineskins' (5:33–39; see Mark 2:18–22). The conversion of Levi is one of the great conversion-stories of the Bible. He was later given the name 'Matthew' (which means 'gift of Yahweh') and was either the author of our Gospel of Matthew or perhaps the author of an earlier version of it.

Levi's sin was great. The tax collectors were a much-hated group of people. They worked for the Roman colonial government and were necessarily intensely disloyal to Israel. They were collaborators with the pagan rulers. They squeezed as much money out of the people as they could. The Romans worked out how much tax they wanted from a particular area and then sold the job of collecting it to the highest buyer. Anything more that the tax collector could get from the people was his to keep. Viciousness and corruption were part of the job.

Levi is a classic example of how suddenly a man may be converted. Jesus leaves the house (mentioned in 5:19). As he is walking along the road he sees Levi at the tax collecting-point. He is actually in the midst of his sin (5:27). In one step Jesus calls him to salvation, to discipleship, and to ministry alongside Himself (5:27). Levi moves from wickedness to ministry in one move. There was no preparation, no preliminary attendance of the synagogue. Actually tax collectors were not allowed in synagogues. The saving grace of God needs no preparation. Our first coming to salvation is like the creation of the world. In the midst of darkness, God says 'Let there be light'.

Levi is a classic example of how salvation turns our life around. When Levi responds to Jesus there is immediately a great change in his life. He abandons his job as a tax-collector (5:28). Immediately he has a great concern to share with everyone what has happened. He is a rich man – as the tax collectors always were. So he uses his wealth to arrange a public banquet. He invites everyone. Other tax collectors are there (5:29). Pharisees are there plus the scribes who are associated with them.

Levi's entire life has been changed around in a few moments. God's grace needs no preparation. When God's grace is at work it achieves miracles in a matter of seconds.

The grace of God offends religious people. There is a difference between faith and what I like to call 'religiosity'. One of the differences is this: religion does not like grace! These Pharisees get upset when they see Jesus being so gracious to men and women like Levi. 'How can someone be saved so quickly?' they say to themselves. 'Why does Jesus associate with such wicked people? Surely they ought to repent first and there ought to be a long period when they clean up their lives before we should associate with such people!' So they rebuke Jesus: *'Why are you eating and drinking with tax collectors and such sinful people?'* (5:30).

Jesus is ready with an answer (5:31–32). He has come for such people. Doctors help the sick! A Saviour saves sinners! God does not work by legalism; He works by grace.

The grace of God creates new ways among the people of God. The next story (5:33–39) is connected with the amazing grace of God that has just been seen in the life of Levi. It begins with a question about fasting. Jesus' critics refer to three 'denominations'. There are the disciples of John the Baptist; there are the Pharisees; and there are the disciples of Jesus (3:33). They are three distinct groups. The two older groups have regular times of fasting, but not Jesus' disciples! Why does Jesus not follow the ways of the other well-known religious movements in Israel?

Jesus gives two answers. First: it is not an appropriate time for fasting (5:34–35). Second: new cloth which has not yet shrunk cannot be used to patch old clothes (5:36). New wine needs new wineskins (5:36–39).

The point of these little parables is that a new work of God needs to express itself in new ways. The amazing grace of God seen in the life of Levi and others is the 'new wine' of the gospel. The gospel of Jesus Christ is ever fresh. God does not change; He is always a God of grace and mercy even to the worst sinner. But the story of the Church of God always has new developments. Jesus is not following the Pharisees. He is not following the disciples of John the Baptist (who it may be noticed have stayed a bit traditional and have kept their own denomination distinct from Jesus' disciples). He is acting directly under God and is doing what the situation requires right now!

Pharisees do not like grace and they do not like newness. But God is always moving us on. The grace of God can act very suddenly. Jesus is simply walking along the roadside when He feels led by the Holy Spirit to summon Levi to Himself. His group of disciples are a new movement in the kingdom of God. They are not simply following the old ways of the Pharisees. They are not even following Jesus' relative and friend, John the Baptist. New wine requires new wine-skins. God is likely to do something new at any moment. We are not under traditions exactly (although they spring up very easily); we are under the direct leading of God. We do not have to follow other peoples' rules about fasting. We go where the grace of God is leading us today!

Chapter 24

Religious People and God's People

(Luke 6:1–11)

The stories about some grain being eaten on the Sabbath (6:1–5) and about a man being healed on the Sabbath (6:6–11) have their parallels in Mark's Gospel (see Mark 2:23–28; 3:1–6).

There is a big difference between religion and faith. Again and again in these gospel stories we discover that 'religious' people get offended with Jesus. Many religious people, even church people, do not have a living fellowship with God.

Take the story in **Luke 6:1–5**. It shows that religious people cannot always tell the difference between big laws and little laws. Jesus and His disciples are walking through the fields on a Saturday, a Sabbath. As they do so, they pluck some grain and start rubbing them in their hands to get to the kernel of the grain (6:1). Immediately the Pharisees accuse Jesus and His disciples of 'harvesting' (6:2); they have in mind the law of Exodus 34:21 which insists that the Sabbath must be kept at harvest-time!

Jesus answers in two ways. First, David in an emergency 'broke the law' about not eating bread inside the sanctuary at Nob. 'Small' laws about ritual and ceremony can be broken when bigger requirements of love and compassion are at stake (6:3–4).

Second, Jesus is 'the Son of Man'. At this point Jesus does not explain what He means by the phrase *'The Son of Man is . . . '*. It could be just a Hebrew way of saying 'I am . . . '. But actually the phrase comes from Daniel 7:13 and soon it will become clear that 'Son of Man' is Jesus' way of talking about His being the Son of God, the Messiah, the fulfilment of

Daniel 7:13. He can break the Sabbath because it is His Sabbath! He reserves the right to change the Mosaic law if He wants to! And He – as the 'Son of Man' – had plans to abolish the Sabbath altogether! He certainly was not planning to be cramped and restricted in life by the legalism and exaggerations of the law that the Pharisees loved so much. Legalistic people generally have a preoccupation about some quite small things. At the time of Jesus the 'Sabbath' was to be kept. One can understand this. The Sabbath was an important part of the Mosaic law. Jesus never broke the Mosaic law, although He certainly broke exaggerations and perversions of the Mosaic law.

But the Mosaic law was about to come to an end. There was something far more important than the Sabbath, and that was Jesus Himself. They are preoccupied about the Mosaic system, but the Mosaic law pointed to Jesus and Jesus is ministering among them. They love the law but they do not love the One that the law points to, Jesus. They want to discuss law; Jesus wants to talk about Himself. The law is not the answer to their need of salvation; Jesus is the answer Himself. His miracles draw attention to the greatness of His person. He is the Son of God. Can they not see it? No, their love of religious law blocks the way to faith in Jesus.

Consider the story in **Luke 6:6–11**. It is another Sabbath day. Jesus is known to heal people. He goes into a synagogue where there is a man with a withered hand (6:6). The scribes and Pharisees are actually looking out for a reason to accuse Jesus (6:7). What sort of religion is this? What is it that fills a person's heart with an eagerness to find fault and cause trouble? Religious people can be utterly blind! How can God be leading them by the Spirit into an accusing spirit?

Jesus knows all about them (6:8a) and He is not bothered! He plans to heal the man anyway. Enemies do not discourage Jesus (6:8b)! As He heals the man He puts a question to them: why are they more eager to keep a holy day than to see a man restored to life and health? Their legalistic ways are destructive. Their religion kills (6:9). He looks around at them all, taking His time and appealing to them. He is not afraid of them. He wants them to consider His words. Their religion is just a blind tradition (6:10a). Then He proceeds with the healing (6:10b). It leads to their being filled with fury and rage. These men with their religion are now plotting to see how they can get rid of this Jesus who upturns their religion and lives for the praise of the glory of God's grace.

Jesus invites the man to faith. 'Stretch out your hand,' says Jesus. I can imagine the man saying, 'But sir that is the one thing I cannot do. I have been trying to stretch out my hand for years. How can you ask me to do such a thing?' But when Jesus gives a command, His power comes with the command! Whatever He commands can be done. Because Jesus has told him to stretch out his hand, he does it, and he finds he can do it! What has been impossible all these years he has done. He has stretched out his hand! What religion and legalism can never do, one word of Jesus is able to perform.

Let us come to some conclusions. (i) Religious people are bothered about laws; God's people live to the praise of the glory of God's grace. (ii) Religious people are bothered about small things; God's people are concerned about 'righteousness and peace and joy in the Holy Spirit' (Romans 14:17). (iii) Religious people are very concerned about sabbaths and 'holy days'; God's people love the Lord of the Sabbath, Jesus Himself. (iv) Religious people put laws above people; God's people learn to be compassionate and merciful. (v) Religious people get angry when their religion is contradicted; God's people carry on regardless – as Jesus did.

Chapter 25

Jesus' School of Discipleship

(Luke 6:12–49)

The first phase of the Galilean ministry (Mark 1:14–3:6; Luke 4:14–6:11) came to a climax when Jesus became popular, and yet was in danger of being killed by the Pharisees (Mark 3:6; Luke 6:11). This perhaps took place in the early part of AD 31. Jesus probably went to Passover in AD 31. About this time **a second phase of Jesus' Galilean ministry begins** (Mark 3:7–6:6; Luke 6:12–8:56). It perhaps takes place in the middle of AD 31. (Some think the dates are three years earlier.) People came from all over the country to hear Jesus, from as far as Idumea in the south, from as far as Tyre and Sidon in the north (Mark 3:7–12). At this point Jesus chooses a high hill among the hills to the north of the sea of Galilee. It is a less populated area and He goes there to pray (6:12), to choose twelve disciples (Mark 3:13–19; Luke 6:12–16), to heal the sicknesses of His followers (6:17–19), and to teach them (6:20–49). Jesus' ministry to His disciples takes place at a lower part of the mountain where there is a level place. There He preaches the famous 'Sermon on the Mount'. It was perhaps a block of teaching which lasted a day or was conducted over several days rather than a single meeting with a single sermon.

The material of Luke 6:20–8:3 has no parallel in Mark's Gospel. The first part tells of the Sermon on the Mount (6:20–49). Then Jesus heals a centurion's servant (7:1–10), raises a widow's son from the dead (7:11–17), answers a question from John the Baptist (7:18–35) and is anointed by one of His followers (7:36–50).

At this time Jesus is misunderstood by His family (Mark 3:19b-21) and is denounced by the Pharisees as having demonic power (Mark 3:22–30). Luke mentions a tour of Galilee made at this time (8:1–3). Because of His rejection by the Pharisees Jesus teaches in parables (Mark 41–35; Luke 8:5–21). Four miracles take place (Mark 4:35–5:43; Luke 8:22–56). Mark mentions Jesus' rejection at Nazareth (already told by Luke) which brings this period to an end. All of this probably took place in middle AD 31. If the feast of John 5:1 is the feast of tabernacles, then Jesus went to Jerusalem in October AD 31 for at least eight days, and the events of John 5:1–47 took place there.

When He got back from Jerusalem there was a further period of Galilean ministry; we shall consider it in a later chapter.

1. **Luke again emphasises Jesus' prayerfulness** (6:12). We have seen that Luke constantly emphasises the value of prayer. He told us how Zacharias' prayer was unexpectedly answered (1:8), and how Anna was called to a life of prayer (2:36–40). He has shown us how Jesus was given the Holy Spirit as He was praying (3:21–22), and how Jesus' fame in Galilee made Him turn to prayer (5:16). Now again we see how Jesus feels the need of prayer.

In Luke 6:12–19, Luke still has Mark's Gospel in mind but he does a little rearranging. Luke specially mentions Jesus' praying on the mountain (6:12). Then he mentions the choosing of the twelve (6:13–16) and the multitudes that were following Jesus at that time (6:17–19). (Mark mentions the multitudes before he mentions the choosing of the Twelve; see Mark 3:7–12; 3:13–19a.)

2. **Jesus trains colleagues** (6:13–16). Jesus has a vision for the future. He is not simply keeping a small ministry moving, He has plans to reach an entire nation and more. When a ministry is to expand it will be necessary for it to increase the number of workers. Jesus is led by God to choose these crucial twelve men who will be the leaders of the work in years to come and will assist in laying the foundations of the churches. He gives them a special name, 'apostles' (perhaps using the Hebrew word *shaliach* or its Aramaic equivalent).

3. **Jesus heals the sick** (6:17). His ministry was a ministry of power, as well as of teaching. God is willing to meet the needs of our entire life. He wants workers who are fit in body and in mind, ready to serve Him. So Jesus heals the diseases of those who have come with Him to the hill country, and He releases them from the power of demons. Sometimes the body has to be attended to before we are ready for spiritual teaching. Luke records that before the famous 'Sermon on the Mount' He brought His Disciples into a state of physical and mental peacefulness.

4. **Jesus guides His disciples in the life of godliness** (6:20–49). Jesus has now taken His disciples aside for a while. The famous 'Sermon on the Mount' is given at this point. It was actually given at a level piece of ground on the hillside (6:12, 17). It was obviously a very lengthy piece of teaching that must have taken at least all day, if not several days. Luke just gives a selection of some of its main points. (Matthew gives a fuller summary in Matthew 5:1–7:29.) Luke's selection includes 'beatitudes' (sayings beginning with 'Blessed . . .') and 'woes' (6:20–26), an extract of Jesus' teaching about love (6:27–36), and a non-judgemental attitude (6:37–45), and he includes Jesus' appeal for obedience (6:46–49).

What exactly is this 'Sermon on the Mount'? It is not a programme for social reform (Jesus is not talking to society at large or addressing the Jewish leaders). It is not an evangelistic sermon. Rather, it is a piece of practical guidance into the life of godliness focusing on matters that need special attention.

Jesus was concerned to train His disciples in the life of godliness. They are not simply managers of an organisation. They are not simply teachers in a school. They are leaders and pioneers in a programme of salvation. Jesus is a trainer of spiritual men who will carry on His work. Part of that training will be training in the life of godliness.

Chapter 26

The Character of the Kingdom

(Luke 6:20–38)

The 'Sermon on the Mount' (as it is generally called) was a lengthy piece of teaching that Jesus gave to His close disciples and followers about living a godly life.

First of all Jesus gives a basic description of the character of the kingdom (6:20–26). **There is blessing in the kingdom of God if its members are free of snobbery and class-consciousness**. The disciple who is truly 'blessed', the person who is happy, the person who is to be congratulated, is described in Luke 6:20–35. Jesus says he or she is poor (6:20), hungry (21a), sorrowful (6:21b) and persecuted for the sake of Jesus (6:22–23)! It is a very surprising way of speaking. Not many people think there can be much blessing in being poor, hungry and sad! Most people dread the thought of being persecuted. Yet such people, says Jesus, experience the kingdom of God (6:20); they are satisfied (6:21a); and they will soon be laughing with joy (6:21b); they will leap for joy at the privilege of suffering for the sake of Jesus (6:23). Is Jesus talking purely about spiritual things or is He referring to literal poverty, and literal hunger? Matthew put the matter more spiritually: *'Blessed are the poor in spirit . . . Blessed are they that hunger and thirst after righteousness'* (Matthew 5:3, 6). Yet it is fairly obvious from a study of the gospels that Matthew and Luke are giving their account of the same 'Sermon on the Mount'.

1. Jesus is not saying that poverty in itself is a blessing. The Bible never says that. Luke does not say 'Blessed are the poor . . .'. He says 'Blessed are you poor . . .'. It is not any poor person who is blessed. It is people like the disciples who

had little wealth yet had trusted their life to Jesus; **those** poor people are blessed.

2. Luke is certainly talking about real poverty and real hunger. Nothing in Luke's words encourage us to 'spiritualise' them. Luke has a special interest in the socially deprived. It is he who tells us of Mary's words: *'He has scattered the proud ... He has filled the hungry with good things, and sent away the rich empty-handed ... '* (1:53). Luke shows special interest in outcasts, in the poor, in widows. The weaker people in society are specially invited to find exaltation in the gospel of Jesus.

3. It is worth remembering that Jesus spoke for a lengthy time but the two versions of the Sermon on the Mount, in Matthew and Luke, take only a few minutes to read. Even in Matthew's report it is clear that Jesus said a lot about worrying over material things and about coveting (see Matthew 6:19–34). Jesus' original preaching obviously was concerned both about spiritual character, and about how poverty and deprivation affect spiritual character. Matthew and Luke are both summarising a lengthy quantity of teaching. Luke's summary concentrates on the way in which financial need can drive us – if we are trusting God – into a deeper experience of the kingdom.

4. Our attitude to the poor people, our experience of need, our attitude to wealth or the lack of it have a lot to do with our experience of the kingdom. Matthew makes these points as well as Luke, but he mentions the matter elsewhere and in a different way. To emphasise the point Jesus put it the other way round. There is blessing for the needy person whose need drives him or her to Jesus. But Jesus predicts misery for the arrogant rich (6:24), the well-fed (6:25a), the person who has no worldly cares (6:25b), the person who is careful to please everyone (6:26).

Secondly, **there is blessing in the kingdom of God if its members are people of love** (6:27–35). Luke is not giving a full report of everything Jesus said; he is picking out the highlights of Jesus' description of the kingdom. Jesus asks us to show love for our enemies (6:27), and to pray for people who mistreat us (6:28). He asks us to 'turn the other cheek', which means to refuse showing resentment or using harsh words in reply to harsh words. When we suffer loss we accept it with a willingness to suffer greater loss (6:29b–30). These instructions are not legislation for society. They are not to be used as part of a national law-code. No society would survive long if it used these words in that way. Nor does it mean that when some con-man wants to defraud us we have to yield to him.

The Sermon on the Mount is not a law-code. It is a description of the attitude, the heart, the spirit, of the member of the kingdom of God. The principle of love is summarised in 6:31. In one sentence: it is treating others the way you wish to be treated. It is only this kind of love that goes beyond the way in which others may live (6:32–33). You can find plenty of nice pagans. They are sweet and kind to their fellow sinners! If Christians are only sweet-natured to others who are sweet-natured, what is so special about that? If you are only generous to people who will repay you, what is remarkable about that? (6:34). Christians are to live at a miraculous level. We are to get to a style of living that can be explained only by the amazing grace of God. We need to be brought by God to a level of miraculous love (6:35) which is practical ('do good'), considerate ('lend'), God-like ('son of the most High'), merciful (6:36), non-judgemental (6:37) and generous (6:38). Perhaps we have not got very far in living such a life. But men and women who know the grace of God in Jesus can live in such a way and Jesus asks them to do so. We need to get there – fast!

Chapter 27

The Wise and the Foolish

(Luke 6:39–49)

The 'Sermon on the Mount' (as it is generally called) was a lengthy piece of teaching that Jesus gave on a hillside north of the Sea of Galilee. Luke picks out some of the highpoints from what must have originally have been much longer. Jesus describes the basic character of the members of the kingdom (6:20–26). Then He calls them to loving, God-like, goodness towards others (6:27–35). Now He warns them to be sharp-sighted and to give attention to the practical obedience to His Word. Luke is summarising that part of Jesus' preaching where He was pressing upon His disciples the need to actually respond to what He is saying. *'A blind man cannot lead a blind man . . . '* (6:39). We remember that Jesus is still on the hillside at the same place where He has just chosen twelve apostles (6:13).

1. **Jesus puts to them the need to be sharp-sighted in order to be leaders of others**. The Pharisees are spiritually blind, but Jesus' disciples must be different. What does Jesus mean by a 'blind man'? He means someone who does not see the need of actually practising Jesus' commands – the kind of things He has been saying in 6:20–39. If Jesus' disciples are to lead others, taking them by the hand and leading them into the kingdom of God, they must be clear-sighted about the things that Jesus has said. Otherwise the leaders and those who are being led will both 'fall unto a pit' – they will both ruin their lives.

Verse 40 continues the thought of verse 39. Christian 'leaders' need to be clear-sighted because 'a pupil does not outrank his teacher'. Jesus is still thinking of the fact that many of His hearers will be the future leaders of His people. They must be clear-sighted in understanding His teaching because their pupils are not likely to be greater than them. (The thought is different from that in Matthew 10:24, 25 where a similar phrase makes a different point.) Those who are trained as Christians in the future will take their pattern from these disciples before Jesus as He is giving this famous piece of teaching.

2. **Jesus' disciples need to attend to their own lives in order to help others**. Jesus uses an amusing picture (6:42). We all have a strange inconsistency in which we can see a speck in another person's eye but are unconscious of a plank of wood in our own! A person with a plank of wood in his eye cannot help others until his own need is met. It is easy to criticise others and want to put them right, but we are not really qualified to do so unless we are able to criticise ourselves first and get our own lives right (6:42).

3. **Jesus presents the need to have a good root to bear good fruit**. *'No good tree bears bad fruit, and neither does a bad tree bear good fruit . . . '* (6:43). The thought continues from verse 42, and is explained in verse 44. One has to have a 'good heart' to truly minister to the other person. After verse 42 it is clear what a 'good man' is; he is one in whom there is no pretence, one who has attended to the needs of his own life. What comes out of the heart of an insincere person will never do much good to others or produce much blessing. The heart is a treasure store. If there are good things within, it will be possible to give out good things for others in what one says.

4. **Finally Jesus challenges His hearers to respond to what He says**. There is a danger about an enthusiastic claim to follow Jesus ('Lord, Lord'), but an enthusiasm which is not matched by detailed attendance to what Jesus says. Jesus explains further with the parable of the two houses. **He is presenting the need to have one's life built on the solid rock of obedience to Jesus** (6:46–49).

Imagine, says Jesus, two men who each want to build to build a house. One is careful about how he does his building. He chooses solid rocky ground on which to build, and digs down to the rock before he starts building. When storms and floods come, the house stands firm. The other man is careless, impatient, eager to get a house up but not careful about how he does it. He grabs the first plot of ground he can find on which to build his house, but does not bother about the fact that he is building his house upon shifting soil. Soon a storm comes and a stream of water overflows near to his house. The house collapses. This is Jesus' picture of how to build our lives on His words. If we are careless we rush to get on with living without taking seriously what He has said to us. If we are wise, we listen carefully to what He says. Then we take action. We dig down to the roots of our lives. Jesus has spoken a lot to us about being truly blessed by relying on God (6:20–26), by being people of love (6:27–38), by being sharp-sighted in attending to the needs of our own lives (6:39–46). The question is: will we dig down deep into the roots of our lives and attend to the words of Jesus? The test comes in the day of a storm. It may be the day of trouble and deprivation. Or it may be a day of judgement. Or it may be the Last Day of judgement altogether. Sooner or later a storm will come and will test the kind of life that we have built. At such a time the only life which will survive is one which has been built upon the words of Jesus the Son of God.

Chapter 28

Spiritual Logic

(Luke 7:1–10)

Jesus finishes preaching on the hillside and returns to Capernaum which was not far away (7:1). There is a Gentile centurion staying there, presumably one of Herod Antipas' solders who came from outside Israel.[1] The Herodian soldiers were organised along Roman lines with centurions. This centurion has a servant who is seriously ill (7:2). He knew about Jesus and had heard that Jesus was in Capernaum. He had believed in the God of Israel and was a supporter of the local synagogue. He asks the elders of the synagogue to approach Jesus requesting healing for his sick servant (7:3). So they come to Jesus on behalf of their friend the centurion, pleading how 'worthy' he is (7:4–5). Jesus starts walking to the house. Some of the elders go ahead to tell the man that Jesus is coming But the man no longer thinks that this is necessary and he sends a message back. Jesus has great authority and this centurion knows all about authority. Let Jesus just say the word and the healing will take place (7:6–8). Jesus is surprised and praises his great faith. The servant is healed (7:9–10). The story is a classic example of great faith.

1. **Some believers have greater faith than others**. There is such a thing as great faith. This man is a believer in the promises of God, but also his faith is greater than usual. Some believers have more faith than others. There is also such a thing as small faith (see Luke 8:25; 2:28).

2. **Faith can grow**. A careful reading of this story shows that this man's faith is growing. He begins by asking Jesus to come (7:3) but then a little later he has more faith and feels even that is unnecessary. Faith can grow as it goes along. Later in

this gospel, the apostles will say to Jesus *'Lord increase our faith'* (Luke 17:5).

3. **Great faith is logical. It rises to great strength by the logic of its arguments**. This is the heart of the matter. What is it that makes faith to be great faith? The answer is: great faith is logical! Listen to this centurion. 'I know all about authority,' he says. 'I am an army officer. I know that one word of authority can get things done. I know that Jesus is a man of authority also. He only has to speak one word, and what He commands will take place.' It is a piece of logical argument. Great faith is always like this. It is logical. We see the same thing in the Syro-Phoenician woman. She also worked out a piece of spiritual logic (as we see in Mark 7:28). Faith looks at God! And then it argues with itself. It says 'I know that Jesus has great authority. I know that Jesus has great mercy – the kind of mercy that will even give a dog some crumbs of food (Mark 7:28). I know that Jesus has all power. I know that He is a man of great compassion. So I reckon – I deduce – that He is able and willing to do this thing for me.' This is the spiritual logic of great faith. Spiritual logic is greater than seeing. The centurion had not seen Jesus. Jesus had not seen him. Nor had Jesus seen the sick servant. It all took place without the major characters seeing each other. The centurion did not need to see Jesus! His spiritual logic was enough for him. He knew that Jesus could do what he was asking and he did not need to see Jesus in order to know it.

The modern Christian is in the same position. We have not yet seen Jesus. We shall do so one day. 'Every eye shall see him'. But at the moment we build our lives not on seeing Jesus in His body but upon our spiritual knowledge. The Holy Spirit had opened the eyes of this centurion without him having to see Jesus. The Holy Spirit does the same for us. Without seeing Jesus we know of His great authority, great mercy, great power. We reckon that He can do anything that is within His will and purpose for us.

4. **Great faith depends on Jesus' mercy**. It is notable that the talk about 'worthiness' does not come from the centurion; it comes from the elders. Maybe that is why the centurion had greater faith than they had! He is not basing his appeal on any

worthiness! He feels most unworthy. 'I am just a Gentile,' he says. 'I am not one of the ones to whom You have specially been sent. I don't even deserve that You should come into my house.' Great faith trusts in Jesus' great mercy. Small faith is afraid to ask God for big things. Often we feel so unworthy that we say to ourselves 'I don't think I could ask God for that!' Yet the thing about this centurion is that he combined great humility with great boldness. He felt utterly unworthy that Jesus should give him anything, but he asked anyway!

5. **Great faith can be found in surprising places**. You would not expect a Gentile to be showing great faith at this stage of Jesus' ministry. Jesus had not yet sent out His gospel to Gentiles. He was ministering only to Jews. This man had a pagan background. He had not grown up among believers. He was a soldier who had been brought into Israel from a foreign country. Yet God can work anywhere and sometimes great faith is found among people that you do not expect to be believers in Jesus at all! Great faith brings great blessing. The servant was healed.

Note

1. Josephus, *Jewish Antiquities* 17:8:3 mentions the nationalities of Herodian soldiers attending the funeral of Herod the Great.

Chapter 29

The Voice That Raises the Dead

(Luke 7:11–17)

There are three occasions mentioned in the Gospels when Jesus raises someone from the dead. This one is the first. The other two are the raising of Jairus' daughter and the raising of Lazarus.

1. **The miracle is a striking instance of the sovereignty of God**. Sometimes God may act in an amazing way just because He wants to and for His own reasons. This miracle was not done because a needy person asked for it (as in 5:12). Sometimes a miracle takes place because someone other than the needy person asks for it (as in 7:1–10). But this miracle took place just because Jesus wanted it to. No one else had the slightest idea it would take place. Here is a person who is totally unknown to Jesus. There is no reason to think that the widow of this story was previously known to Jesus. Soon after the previous miracle Jesus was visiting a city called Nain about twenty-five miles south of Capernaum (7:11). As He is entering the city He passes a funeral procession (7:12). A few questions reveal that a young man has died; he is the only son of a widow (7:13). Jesus is full of compassion for the weeping mother. He touches the stretcher on which the body is laid, covered (one imagines) by a cloth (7:14) and calls the young man back to life (7:14–15). The people are stunned with fear and amazement and instantly hail Jesus as a great prophet and proclaim that a special visitation from God is to be recognised in Jesus (7:16). The news of the event rapidly spreads throughout the 'land of the Jews'[1] and even beyond (7:17). It is one of Jesus' greatest miracles. The woman did not ask for the miracle. As far as we know she was not exercising

any special faith. It was entirely the compassion of Jesus that led to His acting as He did. He acted in the power of His own faith.

2. **When God acts in sovereign freedom it is always a display of His mercy**. God is free to do what He likes, but what He likes is mercy! The miracle-stories of Jesus are always (amongst other things) acted parables. They are literal events; they are samples of what Jesus can do, and samples of what He might do for us. They are attestations of His amazing faith in His Father. They are foretastes of final glory. But in addition to all of these things, miracles are acted parables. They are 'signs' (to use a favourite word of John).

For example, our story gives us a glimpse of the kind of thing God does when He revives the Church. Revival is a powerful, sovereign act of God in which He restores His Church to life and makes it sit up and start speaking for Him. The kind of thing that happened to this young man is a perfect picture of what happens to the Church. Sometimes the Church seems to die. In one area or another it gets weak and sickly and stops speaking for God. But our God is the God of resurrection! Just when the Church seems finally to have died and people are talking about conducting the funeral, God steps in and His Church is raised from spiritual death and starts talking and praising God!

Also, our story is a parable of conversion. The whole human race is like a funeral procession! The wages of sin is death, and every man and woman is proceeding down the road to a funeral – its own. It is a picture that can be applied to the human race as a whole. It moves down the road of life. The whole business is an unhappy affair. There is much pain and sorrow. And at the end of it all there is a funeral and a graveyard. But suddenly – as in our story – there is an interruption. Someone intervenes. Someone – Jesus the Son of God – is deeply distressed at the sorrow that this ugly thing called death brings into the lives of men and women. He calls the whole procession to a halt. With a touch and a word He reverses the pathway to the graveyard. It is exactly what He does in the story of the whole human race. He stepped into our situation. He came into this world to stop a procession of the entire human race to the graveyard. He holds up the entire human race as it parades down the road to doom and death and destruction. He intervenes in the lives of people who are dead in trespasses and sins. When they are in ruin and hopelessness, He reverses what has happened in their lives and gives them the life of God in their lives. He gives them spiritual vitality and the experience of sensitivity towards God. He stops the funeral, and holds it up while He raises someone from the dead. This is analogous to what God did when He saved me, and when He saves you. He stops the funeral, and brings us back to life!

3. **The greatest display of power is seen when death is reversed**. The greatest power there is in this world, other than God Himself, is the power of death. But Jesus' almighty power can reverse even death itself. In a matter of a few seconds a lifeless corpse becomes a living person. What Jesus did to the widow's son He can do in countless calamitous situations. He speaks and the dead are raised. His word is accompanied by His power. When the mighty voice of Jesus speaks, death itself is banished.

Note

1. As elsewhere in Luke, the word for 'Judea' seems to mean 'the land where Jews are to be found'.

Chapter 30

John the Baptist and Jesus

(Luke 7:18–28)

At this time Jesus has been ministering for at least a year. It must be about mid-year AD 31, and about six months after John's arrest and imprisonment. John has been hearing about Jesus but he is puzzled. Like all of the Old Testament prophets John was given a vision of **all** that the Saviour would do in salvation and in judgement. But the judgement has not come; John was not given the sequence of events. John did not know that the judgement could be much later than the salvation. He was not aware that Jesus' first coming would be followed by Jesus' Second Coming centuries later. So he sends a message to Jesus: *'Are you he who is to come or shall we look for another?'* (7:18–20). Jesus does not simply say 'Yes' or 'No'. Instead He invites John to consider the 'signs' of who He is.

1. **He points John to the miracles**. Many people were being healed and delivered from countless ailments and troubles (7:21–22). The miracles are signs of Jesus' very great faith. In the prophecies of Isaiah (see Isaiah 61:1) it was predicted that when God's Servant came He would put bandages on wounded people, and would proclaim release for the prisoners. Perhaps John feels that Jesus is not doing this; he himself is in prison and there is no release for him from his imprisonment! Yet Jesus' many miracles are in fact binding up broken-hearted people and releasing people from many kinds of bondage. But John continues in prison. It is a sign that some have to suffer for the sake of the kingdom. The final triumph of the kingdom has not yet come. Yet the miracles which are

the foretaste of the final triumph ought to show John that Jesus is indeed 'the One who is to come'.

2. **Jesus points John to His preaching to the poor**. One of the greatest indications that Jesus really is the promised Saviour is that He is preaching to the poor (7:22). This is what Isaiah said would be true. 'Yahweh has anointed me to preach good news to the poor'. The gospel of the Lord Jesus Christ is the only message which is really ideal for the totally needy. It says that nothing is needed to endear us to God except willingness to receive His grace. It says that God will give salvation, that the empty hand of faith is the great channel of blessing. It says that the rich have no advantages with regard to the things of God, and the poor have no danger of exclusion because of their destitution. No other message is like it. Jesus selects this relevance of the gospel to the poor as the proof of His authenticity. If our message is not good news to the poor, it is not Christian faith. If our message requires people to be wealthy, or if it is highly suitable to the intellectual or to clever people but has nothing to say to the needy – then it is not the gospel of the Lord Jesus Christ. Conversely, if our message is genuinely and truly an announcement of good news to even the most needy person, it is likely to be the genuine article.

3. **Jesus encourages John to go on believing**. *'Blessed is he who takes no offence at me'* (7:23). John has been troubled by something about Jesus that he does not understand. But he has done one thing right. He has taken his doubt to Jesus Himself! When we have doubts and difficulties about Jesus that is always a good thing to do. Take them to Jesus Himself and let Him answer them.

Jesus' reply is: there is blessing on the person who goes on believing despite a few unanswered questions. One does not need to know the answer to every question in order to trust in Jesus. All of this leads Jesus to say something about John the Baptist and his greatness.

1. **John was notable for his firmness**. He was not a 'reed shaken by the wind' (7:24). He was not a wavering or easy-going person. He was called to preach about sin and repentance. Yet his preaching about the sin of Herod Philip

had brought trouble into his life and now he was in prison. But he was a man who stood firm.

2. **John was notable for his discipline**. He was not a man who lived for earthly luxury (7:25). He did not wear the nice comfortable clothes of people who lived in palaces. God had called him to live a tough and disciplined life. He was not looking for a life of ease or pleasure.

3. **John was a prophet** (7:26a). He was a man who was given what to say by God, like the prophets of the Old Testament.

4. **John occupied a special place in God's salvation** (7:26b). He had the unique task of summarising the message of all the Old Testament prophets. He preached about sin and salvation and made it clear that Jesus was a Saviour from sin, not simply the kind of Messiah that the politicians were hoping for.

5. **John was the last great servant of God before the coming of the kingdom in Jesus** (7:28). Among preachers and prophets no one was greater than John before the coming of Jesus, but he was not in the kingdom of God introduced by Jesus. He was not one of Jesus' disciples, and he was not present on the Day of Pentecost. John was a great man but anyone who came under the ministry of Jesus, who knew of the atoning death of Jesus and experienced the outpouring of the Holy Spirit by Jesus would be in an altogether greater position.

Chapter 31

Changeable Children

(Luke 7:29–35)

When the people heard Jesus speak of the greatness of John (7:28), they 'justified God' – they declared the goodness and righteousness of God. Hundreds of them had been baptised by John the Baptist. It was the specially religious Pharisees who disliked John.

1. **Religious people are often stubborn in rejecting God's good news no matter who brings it**. John had prepared the way for Jesus. Many of the ordinary people had believed in God's Word through John, and they had accepted John's baptism as a sign of their repentance and readiness for God to work in their lives (7:29). Yet the Pharisees and experts in the Mosaic law had refused to be baptised by John (7:30) Jesus says these religious experts were like children in their moaning and complaining (7:31–32). First of all someone plays the flute. But the other children respond 'No, we do not want that joyful happy music.' So instead someone sings a 'dirge' – a funeral song. But they do not like that either! John came. He was called to be a very serious person. He was not famous for loving good food and wine. Far from it. He lived in the wilderness and ate locusts and wild honey. The Pharisees said, 'He is insane, a religious fanatic, an eccentric.' Shortly afterwards Jesus came. He was quite different. The first miracle He did was to create hundreds of litres of diluted wine for a wedding festival! He ate with sinners and drank the diluted wine that was used in those days. He chatted freely with tax collectors and was friendly to sinners. But the religious leaders did not like that either! When someone is determined to pick a

quarrel they will be critical no matter what you do! The religious leaders of Jesus' day rejected John because he did not seem to be very fun-loving. Then they rejected Jesus because He enjoyed life too much and was too friendly! Actually it was not really the seriousness of John or the friendliness of Jesus that offended the Pharisees and the law-experts, it was something else.

2. The truth was, **religious people do not really like to change their mind and admit they are wrong**. What the Pharisees and lawyers did not like was John's message and Jesus' message about repentance over sin. It was Jesus' particular preaching of salvation that really offended them. They did not like the teaching that everyone, even religious people, need new birth and salvation. Unbelief has a negative mentality. When the children in the market-place said to the other children 'Come and dance with us' they were sulky and unresponsive. When the children in the market-place said to the other children 'Come and let's play at having a funeral!' they still were sour and apathetic. Unbelief is never satisfied. Yet the real problem is that the unbelieving leaders of the days of John and Jesus did not like the message of repentance. Both John and Jesus were calling upon the entire nation to repent and turn to God. 'Change your mind! Admit you are wrong! Admit that this worldly ambition of yours is doing you no good,' said John and Jesus to the Pharisees. But the Pharisees would not receive such a message. It did not matter who came. It could be stern John; it could be sociable Jesus. Either way they were offended at the message. Religious people find it hard to change their minds. Their religion is a kind of shield and protection to them – against God! They feel that somehow it will keep them safe. The most difficult thing in the world for religious people is to admit that they need a Saviour to deliver them from sin. Their excuses keep changing! One minute they are saying the gospel is too hard. The next minute they are saying it is too easy! One minute they want to be secular people. The next minute they are thinking that maybe eastern religion has the answer. They can never make up their minds, except that they have made up their minds not to have Jesus! Their excuses change but their unbelief does not

change. Yet what is on offer from Jesus is unchanging forgiveness and the power of God's Holy Spirit.

3. **True wisdom is to be found in the message of John and Jesus**. *'Yet wisdom is shown to be right by all her children'*, says Jesus (7:35). The rightness of God's way of salvation is demonstrated by all those who accept it. This changeable, restless, obstinate refusal to submit to the message of John and Jesus never produces any peace of heart. It is always restless, dissatisfied. But true wisdom will prove itself to anyone who submits to it. True wisdom is to be found in the message of John and Jesus. It begins with an appeal to change our minds, to admit that we are in spiritual need. This was the teaching of John. The people were so interested in a political Saviour, in a mighty soldier who would remove the Roman occupying forces. John said 'You've got the wrong idea altogether. The Saviour who is coming saves you from your own sinfulness. He brings forgiveness of sins. Then He pours out His Holy Spirit upon you.' Those who will accept the message of John and of Jesus will prove for themselves that God's way of salvation is true, and will declare its truthfulness to everyone else. If the Pharisees and lawyers reject the purpose of God for their lives (7:30), the 'child of wisdom' does the exact opposite. The 'child of wisdom' – the true believer – accepts God's plan, discovers that it is everything that it claims to be and boldly tells everyone that he or she has found God's plan to be right and true.

Chapter 32

Forgiven Much, Loving Much

(Luke 7:36–50)

What was it about Jesus that made 'the woman who was a sinner' love Jesus so much? She had not 'fallen in love' with Jesus in a purely biological way. It was her sense of having being forgiven much that produced in her this adoration. She was not simply worshipping God the Father. She was not simply going to church and saying a lot of prayers. She was pouring out adoration and worship towards the Person of our Lord Jesus Christ. The question is: what does this say to us about Him?

1. **Let us look first at Jesus**. He is **sociable**, as always. When invited to a meal, He accepts the invitation (7:36). He is quite **relaxed** and is reclining at a table enjoying the food and talking to Simon the Pharisee when a woman comes in who has a bad name in the town (7:37). Jesus is **wise and knowledgeable**. When the woman comes in, she weeps and then dries Jesus' feet with her long hair (7:38). Simon is shocked (3:29) but Jesus knows exactly what is happening in his heart. He is full of spiritual knowledge. By the Spirit, Jesus senses exactly what Simon is saying to himself. Luke 7:40 says *'Jesus answered him'*, but Simon had not said anything! Jesus knew his heart.

In every situation Jesus is utterly **faithful**. He always does the right thing and says the right thing. He said exactly what needed to be said to Simon (7:41–47), and exactly what needed to be said to the woman (7:48–50).

2. **Let us take a closer look at Simon the Pharisee**. He was **interested** in the things concerning Jesus. He had taken the trouble to invite Jesus to his home. There were a lot of people

around and the door was open for anyone to come in; it was this that enabled the woman to enter the house. Simon was **generous** enough to let his house be used in this way. Some sinners are nice, but when they are being nice we need to remember that they are still sinners. Simon was quite generous, and yet he was **self-righteous**. Nice people are often self-righteous. They may be 'nice' but they know it and feel good about themselves as a result. So Simon feels quite superior to this woman. He speaks scornfully to himself about this sort of woman! (7:39). He does not like the idea of her even touching Jesus. Sinners like her should keep well away from people like Him, he thinks to himself. But this is typical self-righteousness. He is **spiritually ignorant**. Does he not realise that he is a as much a sinner as this woman? He may not have done precisely the things that she has done, but he has the same sinful human nature, And self-righteousness is as loathsome to God as the wickedness for which this woman is known. Simon is **ungrateful**, and ingratitude is hateful to God. Actually he is **unbelieving**. Although he is interested in Jesus and has had sufficient curiosity to invite Jesus to his home, he has not yet come to believe what Jesus is preaching. He has not seen himself as a sinner in need of a Saviour.

3. **Let us look at the woman who loved Jesus so much**. She had evidently lived a wicked life but she had heard Jesus' teaching about God's forgiveness. She knew that in some way He himself was the Saviour and she was so grateful. It was not enough for her that within herself she was thankful; she wanted to do something that showed Jesus how she valued Him and His salvation.

She is **not self-conscious** of what she is doing. She does not care much about what others think. How much time we waste on worrying what others think of us. This woman cared nothing about that! She got a long-necked bottle with perfume or scented oil in it. Then she walked into the house, wanting to stand behind Jesus and anoint His head. Anointing the head was a way of showing respect to an honoured guest. But the woman breaks down in weeping. Her tears fall on Jesus' feet. Ignoring what people think of her, she lets down her hair to dry Jesus' feet. She is not caring at all about what others think.

She is **overwhelmed in gratitude** for what Jesus has done for her. Jesus explains: a money-lender forgives a debtor who owes five denarii, and he forgives another debtor who owes five hundred denarii. Which one will be the most grateful? The one forgiven the most! Simon did not feel very forgiven, but then Simon did not feel that he was a sinner! The woman felt deeply how much Jesus had forgiven her. Of course it was not a matter of the **quantity** of sins she had committed. You don't have to be greatly wicked to feel greatly forgiven! Peter may not have been a specially wicked person when he said *'Depart from me, for I am a sinful man'* (5:8). Yet that was the way he felt. Jesus reassures the woman and tells her she is forgiven. Of course she knew that already! That is the point of the story! She was forgiven already because of her faith (not because of her love). Because she knew that she was forgiven much, she was expressing her love to Jesus. The word of reassurance that Jesus gives her is an **added** assurance. She already knows she is forgiven, but Jesus witnesses with her spirit that she is a child of God. There is such a thing as an **intensified** gift of assurance of salvation, an enlarging of the assurance that one has already. It might be given to us when we forget what others think.

Chapter 33

The Kingdom for the Powerless

(Luke 8:1–15)

Jesus made extensive preaching and miracle-working tours of Galilee as well as making visits outside of Galilee. Early on in His ministry, at a time when great interest was aroused in His teaching and healing, He withdrew from Capernaum and went to other areas of Galilee (Mark 1:38; Luke 4:44). Luke 4:44 to 6:11 has covered this period which took place somewhere in AD 31.

Jesus then spent some time by the seaside area of Galilee (Mark 3:7), and people came to hear Him (Mark 3:8). Soon afterwards, His closer followers went with Him to the hill-country and there on a hillside Jesus gave more teaching to His closer disciples (Luke 6:12–49). There were further miracles after He had left the hills, in Capernaum and in Nain (7:1–17) and a question from John the Baptist was the occasion of some more teaching by Jesus (7:18–35).

Now Luke 8:1–3 lets us know that at about this time there was **a second tour of Galilee in which He took with Him the twelve apostles**. Events on this second tour are reported in Mark 4:1–6:6a, and the material in Luke 8:4–56 covers this time also. There are close parallels especially in Mark 4:1–5:43. Mark also mentions Jesus' rejection at Nazareth (Mark 6:1–6a) which brought this period to an end. Luke does not mention it at the end of Luke 8 because he had put it at the beginning of his story of the Galilean ministry (Luke 4:16–31). He put the bottom line first!

This second tour took place probably in summer AD 31 (or three years earlier as some believe). If the festival mentioned in John 5:1 was the feast of tabernacles in October AD 31, then Jesus was in Jerusalem in October and the events of John 5:2–47 took place.

1. **Jesus was concerned to reach out to a nation**. He went through the towns and villages preaching God's good news (8:1a). He was not a 'pastor' in a single congregation. The work of God requires workers who will attend to peoples' needs in particular areas, but it also needs a more itinerant kind of work, and Jesus' work was of this kind. He was not isolated; He always had people with Him. And it must be said that the modern 'travelling preacher' needs to have a home-church as a base, and churches that are His associates in different parts of the world. No one can be totally 'free-lance', not even Jesus.

2. **Jesus was concerned to work with loyal supporters**. Luke especially mentions the women who were loyal to Jesus (8:2–3). However he mentions the twelve men first (8:1b)! One must not think Jesus only had female supporters, yet it is typical of Luke to give special emphasis to the way in which the less powerful members of society tend to work for the kingdom of God more than the powerful members of society. He pays special attention to Elizabeth, Mary and Anna at the time of Jesus' birth. He alone mentions the widow of Nain, and the sinful woman who showed Jesus much adoration. And we shall find Luke specially telling the events connected with Mary and Martha, and the women at the cross. It is Luke's concern to emphasise that the graciousness of Jesus specially provides help for the victims of the world's injustices. His emphasis on women is part of his interest in God's grace. The men were there as Luke 8:1b shows, but there were women also. Some of them were wealthy and provided financial help. Jesus never had a harsh word to say to any woman, and no woman is mentioned among His enemies. Loyal supporters, men and women, are needed in any work of God. Jesus had some supporters among the poor and the powerless.

3. **The theme of His preaching was the kingdom of God**. This second phase of Galilean ministry included the teaching in parables, and they are 'parables of the kingdom'. 'Kingdom' is mentioned seven times in Luke chapters 1–8. God is a king. He is working powerfully in this world. *'Of his kingdom there*

shall be no end' (1:33). Over against *'the kingdoms of the world'* (4:5), Jesus says *'I must preach the kingdom of God'* (4:43). His teaching clarifies who are the one's who experience His royal power. He says to the poor-but-believing disciples: *'yours is the kingdom of God'* (6:20). John the Baptist was great but anyone who experiences the powerful working of Jesus in his life is greater. The *'least in the kingdom of God'* (7:28) has greater privileges than John because John never remained to experience the miracles of Jesus, His death and resurrection and His gift of the Holy Spirit. On this second ministry-tour Jesus is still *'proclaiming and heralding the good news of the kingdom'* (8:1). Now He shares the parables with His disciples and explains that they will impart *'the mysteries of the kingdom of God'* (8:10).

The most important of the parables is 'the parable of the sower'. Jesus tells the parable to the multitudes (8:4–8a), and then calls out in a loud voice for attentiveness to it (8:8b). His disciples notice the importance of this parable and ask about it (8:9). So Jesus explains. They have a privilege that others do not have. Jesus is offering them the experience of God's kingly power (8:10) but parables are a judgement on those who refuse to hear (8:10). The parable is about responsiveness to God's Word (8:11). The kingdom is given to the disciples but it does not work automatically. It still needs persistent attentiveness. Some get no experience of the kingdom because they have no faith (8:12). Some miss blessing because they fail to persevere (8:13). Some miss blessing because worries, riches and pleasures get in the way (8:14). Hearing, receptiveness, and perseverance are needed to enjoy a rich experience of God's royal power (8:15).[1]

Note

1. For fuller exposition, see Eaton, *Mark* (Preaching Through the Bible), ch. 7 and ch. 8.

Chapter 34

Attending to Jesus' Word

(Luke 8:16–21)

Jesus is concerned to preach 'the good news of the kingdom'.

1. **The kingdom of God comes through attentiveness to His Word** (8:16–18). The parable in Luke 8:16–18 makes the point that Jesus intends that the kingdom of God should be **revealed**. This might seem surprising because the kingdom, says Luke 8:10, is given to some but not to others. For some people the parables are revealing; to others they simply make them more spiritually blind than ever. The parables are 'in order that seeing they may not see'. For those who refuse to heed Jesus the parables are a kind of punishment.

It might seem that God is almost hiding His kingdom. It is a mystery. But Luke 8:15–16 says 'No! God is not **hiding** His kingdom'. God is intending to reveal His royal power. Many miss the experience of God's majestic power but that is their fault, not God's fault. No one lights a lamp and then covers it or puts it in a place where it will not give light. Anyone who lights a lamp will then put it in a place where it can give light to the room (8:16). Similarly God intends His royal power to be known. *'Nothing is hidden that shall not become known . . . '* (8:17). The question is: **when** will the secrets of God's pre-eminent rule become known? For some, it may be known **now** in their own lives and experience. For others, it will be known eventually. This is why Jesus goes on to say, *'Take care how you hear . . . '* (8:18). The experience of the kingdom comes by careful attentiveness and obedience to Jesus. It is still the same message as in the parable of the sower: hearing, receptiveness and perseverance are needed. If we do not respond in this way our experience of the kingdom will lessen. Even that which we think we have shall be taken away. The 'bottom line' of the parable is in verse 18. We must be careful how we hear God's voice. We need to hear Jesus without previous ideas overcoming the power of God's voice. This is specially true when we read the Bible or when we listen to biblical exposition. Often what happens is that we listen to God's Word or we listen to some preaching but we think we already know the truth. We have our own ideas. So when God speaks we put God's Word through a filter and we allow through only what we want to hear. **Take care how you hear**!

We need to hear with a willingness in our heart to be changed. God speaks to us in order to bring about change. Many listen to the Scriptures or to preaching in order to criticise, or to get confirmation of what they already think, or they listen selectively, picking out only what they want to hear. But when we do this it means that we are not listening to God with a view to change, growth and development. God's Word is intended to bring about repentance and repentance involves a change of mind. If we are under God's Word but have already resolved not to re-think anything or not to change our minds about anything, then we are impenitent even before we start! **Take care how you hear**!

Jesus intends that the kingdom of God should be **revealed**. This means that changes and new revelations and new experiences of the power of God in our lives are to be expected every day! Sooner or later, God will reveal the kingdom. But the kingdom is given to some and not to others. If we do not take care how we hear, the parables will not reveal anything to us at the moment. They will actually blind us. They will come to us 'in order that seeing they may not see'. For those who refuse to heed Jesus the parables are a kind of punishment, but then we shall know the truth eventually. One day everything will come out into the open. God's kingdom will be fully revealed. Yet it will be terrible for us if it is only revealed to us **then**. Why should we not experience the power of God's kingdom now? The 'mystery' of the kingdom can be known. It is possible now, in this life, to enter into rich experiences of God's power working in our lives and using us in blessing to others! But everything depends on whether Jesus is able to speak to us. **Take heed how you hear**!

2. **The kingdom of God comes through spiritual relationship to Jesus** (8:19–21). Luke reports at this point that there was a time when Jesus' mother and brothers wanted to speak to Him (8:19). Luke has slightly delayed telling this story in order to link it with the theme of hearing Jesus' Word. In Mark 3:31–35 the story was told a little earlier in the narrative; Luke has rearranged Mark's order of narration. He brings it in here because it makes the point that hearing God's voice has nothing to do with being related to Jesus 'in the flesh'. It does not matter who your parents are or who you are related to. In this matter of experiencing the kingdom, relationships are spiritual not biological. Jesus was told that His earthly family wanted to see Him (8:20). He replied *'My mother and my brothers are those who hear the word of God and do it'* (8:21). Jesus was making the same point as was made in the parable of the sower and the parable of the lamp. The kingdom of God does not come through earthly relationship to Jesus. Even Mary the mother of Jesus could not relate to Jesus in this way. Those who hear and obey Jesus are the ones who are related to Him.

Chapter 35

The Kingdom Which Brings Change

(Luke 8:22–39)

3. **The kingdom of God comes through persistent faith** (8:22–25). Jesus had mentioned persistence of faith (8:13, 15). Luke tells the story of the storm on the lake; it makes the point that faith has to persist even in a storm. Jesus and the disciples are crossing the Sea of Galilee (8:22). Jesus has been busy. He falls asleep in exhaustion. Even a mighty storm does not wake Him up (8:23)! They wake Him up in alarm (8:24), but Jesus asks *'Where is your faith?'* (8:24). If they have truly recognized Jesus as the King of God's kingdom, why have they not attended to His message and held it fast in the middle of a storm? The kingdom of God requires persistent faith. It is those who 'hold it fast and bear fruit with perseverance' who reap its blessings. In their alarm and panic they are not holding fast to their confidence in Jesus. Their experience leads them to a new grasp of Jesus. *'Who then is this?'* they ask (8:25). This event makes them realise He is greater than anything they had imagined! He is one who can be so exhausted that He falls asleep in a boat and not even a storm wakes Him up. But the one who fell asleep with weariness wakes up and commands even the winds and the seas with a single word of command! How can someone be so tired and so powerful at the same time? They are getting a glimpse into the marvels and wonders of the person of our Lord Jesus Christ. He is man as though He were not God. He is God as though He were not man. He has the weakness of a human nature and needs sleep after toil. Yet He has within Him the power of God and when led by the Spirit can, by faith, make use of the resources of the divine nature. By faith

in His Word, by spiritual relationship to Him, and by persistent faith, we shall experience the royal power of God in Jesus.

4. **The kingdom of God overthrows Satan's power** (8:26–33). Wherever the kingdom of God is, Satan reacts with hatred. The kingdom of God is the presence of Jesus as King. Where Jesus is, there is the kingly power of God. When Jesus goes to Gadara[1] there is immediately a repercussion from the world of evil-spirits. Demon-possessed people in the area immediately react. Matthew mentions two of them. Mark and Luke mention one. A man comes with all of the marks of demon possession: nakedness, association with death, recognition of Jesus, fear, violence (8:26–29). Jesus finds out the facts, compelling the demons to reveal themselves (8:30). They ask permission to go into the pigs nearby. Jesus allows them to enter the pigs. It is actually a case of sin destroying sin (8:31–33). God had always forbidden pigs in the land of Israel; they were unclean animals according to the Mosaic law. According to the Bible, animal life may be taken away in situations where the well-being of humankind is more important. This is a situation where the people need to learn something. They need to know God has been displeased with their breaking His law in the land of Israel. They need to know that where Jesus comes such disobedience to the Mosaic law will be rebuked. People will be released from Mosaism eventually but they had not been released yet. Until the death and resurrection of Jesus, God wanted the details of the Mosaic law to be kept. Jesus did not abolish them during His earthly ministry; He fulfilled them.

So an extraordinary miracle takes place. The pigs run down the hill and destroy themselves (8:31–33). Satan is malicious and hateful towards the whole of God's creation.

5. **The kingdom of God requires openness to change** (8:34–39). Now there is a great challenge for the people of Gadara. Jesus has come into their lives unexpectedly. He has revealed that His kingdom is a kingdom of power which destroys the power of Satan. Yet His kingdom will also bring some changes in their lives. If Jesus is tolerated in the land of the

Gadarenes it will not be only pigs that have to go; many other things will have to go as well.

The kingdom of God will bring wonderful things into their land. They can see that the demoniac is now calm and peaceful, sitting listening to Jesus, *'clothed and in his right mind'* (8:34–35). This alarms them! They are amazed to see such an evidence of Jesus' great power. But do they really want Him around to do things like this? The answer is: no, they do not! They prefer their pigs to Jesus. The kingdom of God might be wonderful but they do not want it if it will make them lose their pigs! People are often like this: they beg Jesus to go away so that they might keep their pig-like unclean ways (8:36–37). The opportunity is lost; Jesus goes away. But the healed man will still be among them, proclaiming the wonderful ways of Jesus (8:38–39). Their only hope now will be to heed the testimony of one of God's people. The kingdom of God requires attentiveness, spiritual relationship to Jesus, responsiveness, persistent faith and openness to change.

Note

1. Matthew has 'the Gadarenes' (Matthew 8:28); Mark and Luke have 'the country of the Gerasenes' (Mark 5:1). In all three gospels there are variant readings. It could not have happened in the far-away town of Gerasa. Probably the event took place near Gadara, the regional capital, but the people are called 'Gergesenes' or 'Gerasenes'. Alternatively there was a smaller town on the lakeside with a name like Gerasa, but Gadara was the capital of the area. The complicated evidence is laid out in I.H. Marshall, *The Gospel of Luke* (1978), pp. 336–337.

Chapter 36

A Desperate Woman, a Needy Man

(Luke 8:40–56)

In Luke 8:40–56, Luke is following Mark 5:21–43. Jesus returns to Galilee from Gadara or the land of the Gerasenes' (8:26, 40). When He arrives a crowd are eagerly waiting for Him. A synagogue official named Jairus begs Jesus to come to heal his daughter (8:41–42). As they are going towards Jairus' house a woman suffering from a constant haemorrhage touches the fringe of His cloak and is immediately healed (8:43–44). We read the story with interest. We wonder: will it be possible for Jesus to heal someone without knowing it? No, Jesus says *'I was aware that power had gone forth from me'* (8:45–46). Jesus reassures the woman and continues His journey (8:47–48). Just at that point someone comes with the news that Jairus' daughter has died (8:49), but Jesus tells Jairus not to fear (8:50) and they continue walking towards the house. No one is allowed to witness what happens except those closely involved (8:51). Jesus insists that the girl is only 'sleeping'. Her death is temporary and she will soon 'awake'. But the crowd pour ridicule on Jesus (8:52–53). Soon the girl is raised from the dead but Jesus still insists that the matter be kept confidential (8:54–56).

Both sufferers, Jairus and the woman, had problems which were overwhelming. Both had to persist in faith despite great discouragements. Both were encouraged to continue in faith. And both experienced Jesus' mighty power in their lives. We have considered these matters before, elsewhere,[1] but there are some further principles we can draw from these stories.

1. **Jesus healed by a power that flowed through Him**. The healing could not take place without Jesus knowing it! It was

not just a superstitious reverence for Jesus that brought the woman to health. God let a power rest upon Jesus. When the woman drew by faith from the power that was in Jesus, He instantly knew what had happened. It is a mysterious story and I doubt whether anyone really understands exactly what happened. But it shows that the power was in the person of Jesus. He had to be personally involved and to 'feel' what was happening. It underlines that the answers to our prayers come because Jesus Himself is involved with us and is willing to bless us.

2. **Desperation makes us bold**. The woman was obviously fearful of coming to Jesus in the way in which she did. The haemorrhage she had would make her 'unclean' in the eyes of the religious leaders. But she was desperate. Sometimes God lets things get to a point of desperation in our lives simply because nothing else will drive us to Jesus. Many of us are shy, proud, wanting to hold back and be uninvolved in something that God is doing. But then our situation is so serious that we take steps that we would never take if we were not so desperate.

3. **The woman was not allowed to stay as secretive as she had wished**. Obviously she did not want anyone to know what she was doing. Her faith was secret faith. She wanted no one to know, not even Jesus! She was hoping that she could touch Jesus, get healed and escape without anyone knowing what she had done. Jesus could have let her remain a secret believer. But no, He deliberately makes a point of getting the woman to speak out. The woman had to see *'that she had not escaped notice'* (8:47). People may become 'secret disciples' but Jesus is likely to do something that will bring them out into the open. He knows how to draw us out so that we tell out what has happened to us. After she has publicly acknowledged that Jesus has done something for her, she is given reassurance and sent away in peace (8:48).

4. **Unbelievers are excluded from the greatest of God's blessings**. When Jesus speaks of raising Jairus' daughter the crowd laugh at Him, 'knowing that she had died'. It gives us a typical picture of the world. They are gripped with the sadness of what has happened. They are all weeping and lamenting. It

is typical of the world. They know how to mourn and grieve over death. In many parts of the world, pagans seem to love funerals!

Yet they do not know how to handle the grim reality of death. They think they know all about this world. 'Knowing she had died!' They think they know. They think nothing can reverse the situation now that the girl had died. They send a message to Jesus because they think that now the girl has died it is the end of the matter! When Jesus speaks of His own power they are utterly sceptical and pour their laughter and ridicule upon the Son of God.

One might think that Jesus would show them that they are wrong. So many of us desire to prove ourselves to other people. One might think that Jesus would want to prove to these scornful unbelievers that He can do the very thing that they are ridiculing. He can raise the girl from the dead. But only insecure people have to prove themselves to others, and Jesus is not in the least insecure! He does not at all bring in these unbelievers to witness what He will do. He does the exact opposite. He sends them away and allows no one to witness what He will do except those who are trusting Him in this terrible bereavement.

God does not prove Himself to those who will not believe. He does the exact opposite. For those who believe He will prove Himself! The ones who have persisted in faith see the mighty miracle of Jesus. Those who believe His claims are the ones who experience His power.

Note

1. See Eaton, *Mark* (Preaching Through the Bible), ch. 10.

Chapter 37

Destroying the Works of Satan

(Luke 9:1–6)

There is now a **another tour of Galilee**. We have seen one in Luke 4:42–44 (Mark 1:35–39), and another in Luke 8:1–3. This third mission (Luke 9:1–6), in early AD 32 perhaps, is undertaken by the apostles alone.

1. **The apostles' ministry involved destroying the works of Satan**. The disciples are sent out to extend the mission of Jesus. They are given power and authority over demons and over sicknesses, and they are sent out to preach the powerful reign of God and to heal (9:1–2). What is the relevance of such commands today? Does the Christian Church have authority to cast out demons? Do we heal the sick?

(i) **Miracles and deliverances still take place**. There is no reason to confine Jesus' great and mighty power to New Testament times. His power remains the same. Satan can still be defeated. Sicknesses may still be healed.

(ii) Yet, **modern Christians must not pretend they are experiencing power on a level with what happened in New Testament times**. The story of the Church is not ended yet! There may come an age in the Church which is even greater than that of the first generation. But meanwhile we must not make false claims. So far, no one seems ever to have had anything near the power that Jesus and the apostles had. Jesus healed directly with a word or with a touch. Jesus' miracles were instantaneous. On one occasion when He had a reason for performing a miracle in two stages, both stages were instantaneous. The healings were always complete. The miracles were dramatic rather than trivial. A severed ear was instantaneously replaced. Limbs were instantaneously repaired. Organic diseases were instantly banished. There is no known case where there was a relapse back into the sickness. A whole village could bring its sick and everyone would be healed. Jesus on one occasion stopped a funeral and raised the boy whose funeral was taking place. A man who had died several days previously was raised after being buried in a tomb. No one has a track record like that!

Jesus' command to His apostles points our faith in the right direction. God gives miracles of deliverance and gifts of healing but the authentic miracles are only present in small measure – at the moment! We look for more but we make no claims until they are obviously justified. The miracles of Jesus' day were indicators of His authenticity, samples of what Jesus can do for us, parables of what He is able to do at a deeper level, and they are foretastes of the resurrection. Since the Church is commanded to do all that the apostles did (Matthew 28:18–20) we may look to God to bless us in this way, but we must not over-claim. Certainly the basic character of our work is the same: we are called to destroy the works of Satan.

2. **The apostles' ministry involves the preaching of the kingdom**. The Greek word 'preach' in this verse[1] means 'to proclaim' or 'to do the work of a messenger speaking out a message in a central place where the people are to be found'. It is not quite the same word as 'teach' which refers to the detailed explanation of a largish quantity of skills and information.

3. **The apostles' ministry was accompanied with obvious simplicity of life** (9:3). They were not to go with a vast quantity of supplies, provisions and luxuries. They should not give the impression that being involved in Jesus' mission to Israel was a highly enriching business. They were to take just what they had and to look for God and His people to help them along their way. They were to take nothing for the journey. They were not to acquire a spare purse or a new purse.

The point of these instructions was that the apostles were to live simply, in dependence on God and on His people. They may take what they have but should take nothing **extra** because Jesus would see that they were given sufficient supplies along the way. No new staff should be obtained. No new sandals should be obtained. No new money bag should be acquired.

This does not mean they should not take staff or sandals or purse at all! Mark's account makes it clear that they were allowed to take what they had including a staff. But no new sandals or new equipment were to be bought. The apostles were to be ordinary people with ordinary supplies; God would maintain them. These instructions would change later in Jesus' ministry when they were sent **outside** Israel. But at this point when they are being sent to God's people, they may expect God's people to be a means of supply to them.

4. **The apostles should make a simple base for their work wherever they went**. *'Whatever house you enter, stay there'* (9:4). It means that when someone offered them hospitality they should make that place their base. It would give a false impression and be excessively tiring to stay in one home after another in the same area.

5. **The apostles should not be troubled when they are rejected** (9:5). If they discover that in a certain place they are unwelcome they are simply to go elsewhere. They leave behind the dust of their shoes to testify that they were there! This language is playful. It is a way of saying that they have discharged their responsibility and need not be troubled any further.

These instructions were followed by the apostles (9:6). Although not every word is literally applicable to the modern Christian, yet they still retain much wisdom and the basic charge remains the same: we are to destroy the works of Satan and announce that God's royal power is here!

Note

1. The word is *kerusso*.

Chapter 38

Walking With Jesus

(Luke 9:7–17)

As a result of the preaching and healing of the apostles throughout Galilee, Herod Antipas, the ruler of Galilee, gets to hear about the ministry of Jesus (Mark 6:14–16; Luke 9:7–9) and fears that Jesus is John the Baptist back from the dead. This section of the story draws our attention to four immensely valuable privileges that comes to those who walk with Jesus.

1. **A good conscience**. Jesus and His disciples are men with clear consciences, but Herod Antipas has to live with a bad conscience. Life is not easy for Jesus. Soon He will be almost daily seeking to avoid Herod Antipas. Herod wants to see Jesus, but Jesus does not want to see him! John the Baptist had spoken often to this man Herod and had rebuked him for marrying Herodias who had been the wife of his brother Herod Philip, son of Mariamne. As a result of his rebuking Herod Antipas, John had been put in prison and then had been executed. But now Herod hears of someone who is preaching the same message as that of John the Baptist, the message concerning the kingdom of God. Now Jesus is in danger from Herod Antipas but has the joy of knowing He has a clear conscience. Herod is a powerful person but he lives with the knowledge that he killed John the Baptist. Conscience is a powerful aspect of our personality. It does not in itself bring us to salvation, and it can be misguided, but the conscience is a influential voice within us and can give us peace or can make us highly superstitious and nervous. Jesus was in danger but had much peace. Herod was powerful but had no peace.

2. **Fellowship with Jesus** (9:10). Mark gives us now the report of the disciples returning from their two-by-two mission (Mark 6:30–31; Luke 9:10a). The disciples go to the eastern shore of the Sea of Galilee. Fellowship includes the privilege of telling Jesus everything that has happened to us. *'And when they had returned the apostles told him all that they had done'* (9:10). They had been telling out the message of the kingdom and had no doubt healed many people. Now they come back eager to tell Jesus what they have done. No doubt they had made mistakes. Perhaps some villages had rejected them. Now they have the privilege of telling it all to Jesus and receiving His comments and advice.

It includes the privilege of spending time alone with Jesus. *'And taking them away with himself he withdrew privately to a town called Bethsaida'* (9:10b). It is a good thing after we have been exceptionally busy to take a break to be with Jesus. The apostles did this physically; we do the same thing but our contact with Jesus is 'in the Spirit'. We need time to think and pray and become conscious of God's presence.

3. **Ministry with Jesus** (9:11). The little holiday with Jesus did not last very long! Jesus was always much in demand. Often when He turned aside to rest people would follow Him. This did not seem to trouble Him very much. Even when He withdrew into privacy people came looking for Him but He always had time for them. People followed Him to Bethsaida and He talked to them informally about the kingdom of God, and healed those of them who were sick. He was more willing to teach than people were to be taught. He was more willing to help than people were to believe. For the disciples it meant the privilege of learning to be always ministering to people. For many people 'rest' means withdrawing totally from people, but Jesus does not seem to have thought of 'rest' in quite this way. He did not find people a strain upon Him. He withdrew from tumult and turmoil but He did not mind if some people followed Him and He was always ready to help them.

4. **Provision from Jesus** (9:12–17). The number that followed Jesus were not few. The feeding of the five thousand takes place at this point and that means that there were

thousands who followed Jesus on His 'holiday'. The apostles speak to Jesus about the need of the people (9:12). He says *'You give them something to eat!'* (9:13). It is worth noticing that before Jesus performed the miracle of the feeding of the five thousand He invited the apostles to do it! If they had responded in faith to His instruction they could have fed five thousand people with miraculous provision. But they thought only about their limited resources (9:13). So Jesus takes control. The people sit down in groups (9:14–15). Jesus likes to do things decently and in an orderly manner. The five loaves and two fishes are distributed and an amazing miracle of provision takes place (9:16–17). It is one of the most amazing things He ever did, and has never been exactly repeated since He did it. Never has there been such an undoubted miracle of creation indisputably experienced by thousands of people. Even unspiritual people could not doubt that it had taken place.

It was designed to teach the people that Jesus was the Creator, and the King of the universe. He could abundantly provide for all of His people. He could meet any need of theirs at any time He wished. So abundant was His provision He could create enough for twelve baskets of surplus food. Any one of the five thousand could have had more if he wanted!

There is an abundance of resources and supplies in Jesus. Anyone truly in His plan will not lack His supplies. Nothing is impossible for Him. It is a lesson for the apostles – and for us – that amidst the needs and distresses of the world that surrounds them they have a Saviour who can do anything.

Chapter 39

The Saviour and His Cross

(Luke 9:18–27)

Luke passes over some events that are recorded in Mark's Gospel. Mark tells of the miracle of walking on the water (Mark 6:45–52). Jesus visits the area in and around Bethsaida; then He crosses over the lake and performs many healings at Gennesaret (Mark 6:53–56). This must have been round about Passover, April AD 32. When the Pharisees come to Jesus the major exposition concerning the 'traditions of the elders' takes place (Mark 7:1–23). At this point there came a temporary withdrawal from public ministry (see Mark 7:24). Jesus went to Tyre. In Phoenicia, the Syro-Phoenician woman gets her request answered (Mark 7:24–30). Jesus then goes through Sidon, the Sea of Galilee, and the Decapolis. He heals a deaf mute (Mark 7:31–37), the four thousand are fed (Mark 8:1–10). Then Jesus crosses to Dalmanutha and Magadan (Matthew 15:39) perhaps on the east coast of the Sea of Galilee, and the Pharisees seek a sign (Mark 8:11–13). While crossing the Sea of Galilee, Jesus warns His disciples against them (Mark 8:14–21). A blind man is healed at Bethsaida (Mark 8:22–26). At Mark 8:27 and Luke 9:18 the two gospels come together again. *'As Jesus was praying alone, His disciples were with Him'*, says Luke 9:18. It is another proof that Jesus did not find people distracting. He could be 'alone' in a crowd.

Who is able to recognise Jesus as the Son of God?

1. **A vague admiration for Jesus is insufficient**. Jesus asks what are the opinions of the common people concerning Himself (9:18). Some think Jesus is John the Baptist. Others thought that Jesus was Elijah or one of the prophets (9:19). It

seems that people generally admired Jesus and thought He was some kind of prophet on the model of the prophets of days gone by.

Many people think Jesus is a good person and have a vague and general admiration of Him. Yet a vague admiration for Jesus is not enough. Jesus not only comes with teaching which we should admire, He also makes claims about Himself.

2. **True disciples come to an altogether greater conviction about Jesus**. Jesus asks the disciples what they believe (9:20). Peter replies for all of them. The disciples have come to know that Jesus is the Messiah, the predicted King of Old Testament prediction. Jesus is the unique divine Saviour. There is no one else who is the one-and-only fulfilment of the Saviour predicted for Israel and the world. Jesus is uniquely empowered. There were predictions in the Old Testament saying that God's coming Saviour would be specially empowered by the Holy Spirit. It was for this reason that the coming Saviour came to be known as 'the Messiah', 'the Christ', 'the Anointed One'.

3. **Others must come to recognise Jesus by faith**. When people come to believe that Jesus is the predicted Saviour, He does not encourage them to speak too loudly about the matter (9:21). One obvious reason is that people had a very worldly idea of what the Messiah would be like. If Jesus simply says 'I am the Messiah' or if others say 'Jesus is the Christ', most people will interpret the claim politically. People are very eager to have Jesus on those terms.

4. **Faith must reckon with the cross of Jesus**. Jesus takes His disciples aside and tells them *'The Son of Man must suffer'* (9:22). This was hard for them to take. They were very used to the idea of a Messiah coming in glory, but the idea of a suffering Messiah was not something they could take to easily. But it was not only a matter of reckoning with the cross in the life of Jesus. Jesus goes on to say that if they wish to get to glory and honour following Jesus [1] they must (i) deny themselves, (ii) take up their cross daily, and (iii) follow Jesus. They must reckon with the cross in their own lives as well as in the life of Jesus (9:23).

Denying ourselves is a matter of denying our own instinctive sinfulness; saying 'no' to our self-centredness, our love of certain sins, and resisting the *'sinful nature with its desires'* (Galatians 5:24).

'The cross' may be any chastening which Jesus imposes on us, which is painful and 'crucifies' our love of sinful ways. Our gospels only give hurried summaries of what must have been a lengthy conversation. Luke knows that part of the matter is the **daily** crucifixion that the Christian must accept. Luke has the word 'daily'; the other gospels do not.

Every day there will be things coming across our path which will 'crucify' us. There will be times when we have to swallow our pride, times when comfort and pleasure eludes our grasp, frustrations which run across our desire for an easy life.

5. **Self-denial and crucifixion is the only way to gain life**. Jesus still has these matters in mind when He goes on to say, *'For whoever would save his life will lose it . . .'* (9:24). Some will seek to hold on to 'life', the easy life that refuses the self-denial and crucifying experiences that are necessary to our 'coming after' Jesus. Such people lose 'life' – the liveliness that comes by the presence of God, the rich rewards of God's presence, peace and power. It is a poor exchange. The world might be gained, but the life that comes from God is not experienced (9:25). Better to lose a few fleshy comforts and gain the life which is life indeed. Better to acknowledge Jesus now than to be unacknowledged by Jesus (9:26). Soon the kingdom of God will come with power (9:27 refers, I believe, to the exhibitions of the kingdom of God in the outpouring of the Spirit and the fall of Jerusalem). The time for self-surrender is now.

Note

1. For fuller exposition, see Eaton, *Mark* (Preaching Through the Bible), ch. 18.

Chapter 40

Jesus' Glory Revealed

(Luke 9:28–43a)

Mark and Luke are now running side-by-side. Luke 9:18–36 is parallel to Mark 9:2–10. Luke 9:37–50 follows Mark 9:14–41. We have now the stories of the transfiguration (Luke 9:28–36) and the demon-possessed boy (Luke 9:37–43a).

About eight days after the events at Caesarea Philippi (9:28) Jesus and three disciples went to a mountain to pray, and Jesus is transfigured before them.

1. **It was a confirmation of the need for prayer**. It is typical of Luke that he alone emphasises the purpose of the trip was to pray, and it was as Jesus was praying that the transfiguration took place (9:29).

2. **It was a confirmation of their faith in Jesus**. Having come to faith in Jesus' Messiahship without any experience such as this one, their faith is now confirmed by something that they see.[1]

3. **It was a preparation for suffering**. The disciples receive a glimpse of the honour that attends Jesus as the divine Son of the Father. But also there immediately follows a conversation concerning Jesus' death in Jerusalem (9:30–31). Jesus was given an amazing opportunity to talk to the heroes of the days of the Mosaic covenant. He talks to Moses, the representative of the law and the founder of Israel. He talks to the greatest of the prophets, Elijah. It is His **death** that is the topic of conversation. The triumphant Son of Man whose glory is shining out visibly must suffer! It was a visible proof that Jesus' death would be the fulfilment of the law and the prophets.

4. **It was an assertion of Jesus' uniqueness**. The disciples wish to prolong the occasion. *'Let us make three tents, one for you, and one for Moses, and one for Elijah'* (9:33). But the experience will not be a long one and booths will not be necessary. The suggestion is also putting Jesus on a level with the others: 'Jesus ... Moses ... Elijah' – as if they are equals. It is the same mistake that was made by the common people: 'Jesus ... John ... Elijah ... one of the prophets' (9:18). But a cloud denoting the divine presence comes down (9:34), and God's voice directs their attention to Jesus only (9:35), underlining His person ('my Son'), His work ('my Chosen One') and His authority ('Listen to him!'). Moses and Elijah are nothing compared to Jesus the Son of God (9:36).

Again the disciples do not speak of their experience. People are to come to faith by the enlightenment of the Spirit, not by hearing a strange and impressive story of glory appearing on a mountain

5. **It was a preparation for ministry**. The next day the disciples return from the mountain (9:37). Almost immediately they meet with a practical difficulty of ministry. A demon-possessed boy has been brought to the other disciples but they have been unable to help (9:38–40). It is unbelief that is the cause of the failure (9:41). The case is a severe one (9:42) but Jesus heals the boy (9:42b) and everyone marvels at the power of God (9:43a).

Jesus did not stay long on the mountain. His experience with visitors from the heavenly world was a rare privilege even for Jesus. And it was only something to strengthen Him and His disciples for the practical challenges that would face them in the work of God. The greatness of Jesus' divine glory is shown us side-by-side with the greatness of the human predicament. Even Jesus was distressed by the greatness of unbelief. The question now is: will the disciples profit from what they have seen of Jesus' glory? They were looking for glory but had been warned about suffering. As soon as they come down from the mountain there is a case of great suffering in front of them. And Jesus is in distress because of the unbelief of His disciples and followers. But the glory they have just experienced should sustain them amidst the practicalities of serving God. The experience of glory is not given them just to be a religious experience. Nor did it last a long time. It is something that will make them know that Jesus is authentic, and that they can trust Him as the Son of God amidst an unbelieving world and demonised sufferers.

They were wanting the honour of an earthly kingdom, but instead will have the honour of ministry. Peter had wanted to build some kind of structure of the top of the mountain so that they could stay there and enjoy the delights of conversation with Moses and Elijah. But instead of talking theology with Moses and Elijah they are being asked to give help to people like the distressed father and his demonised son. The kingdom that Jesus has brought into this world does not have much glory in it just yet. The glory is coming! The disciples are allowed some foretastes of it. But that is only to sustain them. For the moment they are not being commissioned to be ministered unto but to minister to others. It is not yet a kingdom of visible glory. It is a kingdom of ministry to the needy and the demonised.

They had shown foolish interest in holding on to a great experience, but instead Jesus is inviting faith. 'O unbelieving generation!' said Jesus. The remaining nine disciples had been unable to help the child because of the weakness of their faith. Now Peter, James and John have seen an appearing of the divine glory in Jesus. They have spent time in prayer. They have received an unshakeable revelation of the majesty of Jesus. Will they **now** have the kind of faith that Jesus is wanting? Great experiences of God's glory are only intended to increase our faith and enlarge our capacity for serving God and His kingdom.

Note

1. See fuller exposition in Eaton, *Mark* (Preaching Through the Bible), ch. 19.

Chapter 41

The Marks of Greatness

(Luke 9:43b–50)

Jesus is increasingly warning His disciples that His work in this world involves His going to the cross to die.

1. **Jesus' greatness focuses upon the cross**. There is emphasis on the cross in all of the four gospels. In the Gospel of Luke, the first hint of the cross was in Luke 6:11. There we had our first warning that the Jewish leaders were planning to do Jesus harm. After the confession of faith at Caesarea Philippi, Jesus begins to be more explicit in predicting His death. *'The Son of Man must suffer many things . . . and be put to death, and . . . be raised'* (9:22). Now Jesus gives a second prediction. *'The Son of Man is about to be delivered into the hands of men . . .'* (9:43b–44). We are less than half way through the gospel and yet the death of Jesus is already being heavily emphasised. Imagine you were writing a biography of someone who lived until he was about thirty-three years old. Would you be dealing with how he came to die when you were less than half way through the biography? Probably not. This shows us how much emphasis there is on the death of Jesus. They did not yet understand what He was saying (9:45). Not until the Holy Spirit was poured out upon them would they come to a clearer understanding. Then on the Day of Pentecost the death of Jesus would come clearer to them in a matter of seconds. But whether they understand or not Jesus goes on telling them about His cross. They will understand one day. After the day of Pentecost these predictions will come back to their memories and they will realise that all along the way Jesus was talking to them about His cross.

2. **Greatness is seen in freedom from snobbery**. 'Snobbery' is social pride, a feeling of superiority that comes from our being in a wealthier or more eminent position in society. The disciples are very interested in being eminent in society. They have heard Jesus speaking of the kingdom of God. They still think very much in terms of the Romans being expelled and Jewish leaders ruling the nation. They are eager that they should have important parts to play in this new kingdom. Little do they know what the future holds for them! They are already discussing which disciples will have the greatest authority (9:46).

Jesus calls a child to be near at His side (9:47). His reply to the disciples has two parts to it. Firstly, greatness is revealed in the people you are willing to **receive**. Most people would not pay special attention to children because they are powerless and they are not wealthy! The disciples are already thinking of how great they will be. They are interested in the important people they will have in their kingdom. Jesus says the mark of greatness is to have an interest in the poor and powerless. The child is a sample of social powerlessness. Jesus has come for such people.

The second part of the reply deals with their own willingness to take a lowly position. **He who is least among you is the one who is great**. Like all of Jesus' teaching it deals with attitude; it does not makes absolute rules. Freedom from self-assertiveness is the mark of greatness. A child is dependent on adults. He or she has no great status, but is under the authority of parents or guardians. The person who is child-like does not strive for power. The one who has child-like dependence on God, child-like readiness to let God's will take place, such a person is great in the kingdom of God. Any disciple who wants to be 'great' has lost greatness already! The one who will be great in God's sight is the one who, like a child, is not bothering about greatness at all.

3. **Greatness is seen in freedom from rivalry**. The disciples hear of a person who casts out demons in the name of Jesus. He does not belong to the twelve apostles or any of those who travel with Jesus. It is rather like the story in Numbers 11:24–30. The disciples react with indignation. It is typical of all of

us that we want people to be in our group. Human beings are generally somewhat hostile to other cultures, other nationalities, other tribe, other denominations. This exorcist evidently had a high regard for Jesus and used His name in his work. The disciples were indignant that he was not fully submissive to their little group of disciples led by the twelve apostles. Denominationalism is starting already!

There is a link between what Jesus says here and the previous section. Their desire to be the only people who represent Jesus is part of their desire for worldly greatness. They would love to forbid anyone serving Jesus unless He does so under their banner. Then they will feel more important!

But Jesus feels quite differently. He does not mind if someone has learned a little about Him and is seeking to minister to people in His name – even if that person is being rather independent-minded. 'He that is not against you is for you'. There will be plenty of people crying out 'Crucify Him! Crucify Him' in a few months after this time. People who are more on our side than against us are to be welcomed!

This is what true greatness is: recognition of the cross of Jesus, a willingness to let vindication and social eminence come from Jesus alone, and a loving, gracious, large-hearted approach to everyone everywhere. To become like this is itself a 'crucifying' experience. This is what Jesus meant: 'if anyone wishes to come after Me let him . . . take up his cross – daily.'

Chapter 42

Moving Towards the Cross

(Luke 9:51–62)

Luke 9:51 to Luke 18:14 is distinctive to Luke's Gospel. It is a 'travel narrative'. As Jesus travels He ministers to the people of Israel and teaches His disciples.

Jesus is ready to die in Jerusalem. He travels there by a twisting and turning route (avoiding Herod). The journey to Jerusalem is emphasised three times in these chapters (Luke 9:51; 13:22; 17:11) but it is all the same journey. Whether Luke 9:51 to 18:14 is in chronological order or not is debatable. It is not easy to tell whether Luke has altered the order of events to put stories of the same kind side-by-side. Certainly everything in 9:51 to 18:14 happened at some stage on the lengthy journey to Jerusalem. Judging from Luke's use of Mark elsewhere, it is likely that Luke 9:51–18:14 is basically in chronological order but there might be a few events told out of order so as to put similar material together.

1. **The central purpose of Jesus' earthly life is to go to Jerusalem to die**. Verse 51a says *'And it came about, when the days were approaching for Him to be received up, that He set His face to go to Jerusalem'*. The Greek for 'received up' is a word that often refers to death, but there can be no doubt that it includes the idea of Jesus' being 'taken back' to God's presence, just as Elijah was 'taken up' into heaven (note the reference to Elijah in 9:54, which echoes 2 Kings 2:1, 10, 12). Jesus knows that He is being 'taken up' to His Father via His death upon the cross.

Jesus Himself knew from early days in His life that He had come into this world to die. His baptism was a call to die for sinners. The voice from heaven called Him to be the Suffering

Servant of the predictions of Isaiah. At Caesarea Philippi He told the disciples that He must be killed and after three days rise again. Now He is on His last journey to Jerusalem. He knows what is to happen to Him. Yet He was determined to give His life as a ransom for many.

What amazing dedication we find in Jesus! How determined He was to do God's will, even at the cost of immense suffering.

2. **The cross of Jesus was part of His plan not to judge sinners but to save them**. He is travelling towards Jerusalem. On the way He enters a Samaritan village but they reject Him because they hear He is going to Jerusalem (Luke 9:52–53). There was a terrible hatred between Samaritans and Jews. The Samaritans hated Jerusalem; they had a corrupt and twisted version of the faith of the Old Testament. 2 Kings 17:24–34 tells the story of their beginnings. But the opposition of the Samaritans did not distract Jesus. The cross is more important to Him than His relationship to the Samaritans; He keeps travelling to Jerusalem. James and John are indignant. Imagining Jesus to be like Elijah they feel they should call fire from heaven, as Elijah did according to 2 Kings 1:10–12. How strange that Jesus should be going to the cross to save sinners, but His disciples are eager to call judgement down upon sinners. Jesus did not come to judge sinners. James and John were at this stage of their lives 'sons of thunder' (Mark 3:17), but Jesus *'did not come to judge the world, but came in order to save the world'* (John 3:17).

The cross in Jesus' life must become the cross in the disciples' life. He is walking to the cross to save Samaritans and He will single them out for special blessing ('and Samaria', Acts 1:8). Jesus loves Samaritans; the disciples must learn to have Jesus' love in their attitudes. Otherwise they miss the point of Jesus' cross.

3. **The cross of Jesus invites our discipleship**. One of Jesus' followers is very eager to follow Him. *'I will follow you wherever you go'*, he says. It is important to remember that 'following Jesus' was a quite literal matter. It was a matter of becoming a 'trainee' in the work of the kingdom by travelling with Jesus to learn to do what He did.

The man is too eager. He needs to face the fact that there is hardship and suffering in following Jesus. Jesus has no home of His own (9:58) and there will be no luxuries for followers of Jesus. Today's disciples need to remember the same point: there are few luxuries for those who go all the way with God – only the delicious joy of having His approval.

Another man is the exact opposite to the first. Jesus invites him for training and ministry in His kingdom (9:59a), but the man wants to delay ministry until after his father has died (9:59b). Jesus' answer is: people who are spiritually dead must at times be left to take care of their own affairs; disciples cannot delay obedience because of them (9:60). Actually Jesus' death is itself only a few weeks' away. Jesus will probably die before the father!

Another would-be disciple is the exact opposite. He has been with Jesus thus far, but now he wants a period with his family before he commits himself to a further step (9:61). Jesus sees that he is simply reluctant to go any further in serving God. *'No one who puts his hand to the plough and looks back is fit for the kingdom of God'*, He says. Anyone who becomes a believer and starts serving God, 'putting his hand to the plough', but then starts drawing back will lose out in his experience of the kingdom. This is not a statement about salvation (for salvation is by faith not by 'putting one's hand to the plough'). Rather it is about fruitfulness and reaping the full blessings of the kingdom of God.

Chapter 43

Helpers in the Work

(Luke 10:1–16)

As Jesus travels towards Jerusalem, He appoints seventy-two co-workers to go ahead of Him (or perhaps seventy; the manuscripts vary). They will announce Jesus' message and His coming visit to them.

There are some things that are unique about the sending out of the seventy-two workers; later on some of His instructions would be changed (see 22:35–38). Yet there is also much that we can learn about our own calling as Jesus' disciples today.

1. **Our task in this world involves outreach**. This is perhaps the main lesson we should learn from this section of Luke. Christians are not are to be static and motionless in their outlook on life. Not every Christian is called to be a traveller in the way in which these disciples were, and some may be called to stay in the same country and town all of their lives. Yet every Christian is called to have an outward-looking attitude and to be involved in some way in following the pattern of sharing the powerful kingdom of God with the entire world. Jesus was never stationary. He moved around Israel. As soon as possible He called twelve to extend the message of the kingdom. Now He sends out seventy-two. Soon He will be speaking of reaching the entire world (Acts 1:8). The entire sweep of Luke–Acts is a story of the steady expansion of the influence and activities of God's rule in this world. God does not intend the extension to stop until '*. . . these last days*' (Hebrews 1:1) come to an end and Jesus comes to introduce a new phase in the story of His people.

Although not everything in this narrative can be simply transferred to the modern Christian, yet some of it can, and the call to enterprise and zeal in extending God's reign and rule applies to every Christian.

2. **Jesus gives us some practical help in knowing how to extend His reign**. The disciples are to go out as thirty-six pairs of workers (10:1). Isolation in such a work would be risky. They are to pray for the number of workers to increase. The task is a very big one and as they go they are to pray for helpers in the work (10:2). They are to realise that the work will at times be dangerous. They are like lambs among wolves (10:3).

They are to travel light. They carry no cash, no spare equipment or provisions. They must trust God for everything. It is only a brief mission. Soon Jesus will be giving them fresh instructions (see Luke 22:35; Acts 1:8). They are not to waste time giving formal courtesies to people they meet. They are to be polite obviously, but must not waste time on lesser things (10:4).

They are to act with respect, but with a sense of authority. When they arrive at any area they begin by calling upon God to give His peace to that place (10:5–6a), but if they are unwelcome, the offer of God's peace will be withdrawn (10:6b). They will make one place their base (10:7), and enjoy its hospitality for their short stay (10:8).

3. **Jesus defines the nature of their work**. They will pray for the sick and announce God's kingdom (10:9). It is not a complicated matter. They are not to be learned scholars or highly organised directors of great projects. They simply announce that Jesus is God's Messiah and the possibility of experiencing Him as their king is right there for any who receives their message. If they are not welcomed in any particular town or village they must leave (10:10–11). The basic message they take with them is that of God's kingdom. We have noticed before the centrality of 'the kingdom' in Jesus' ministry. God is willing to come into our lives and into our society and act as King among us. In Luke chapters 9–11 the kingdom of God is mentioned another eleven times (9:2, 11, 27, 60, 62; 10:9, 11; 11:2, 17, 18, 20).[1]

It is to be preached (9:2, 60) and spoken about (9:11). Its power is displayed visibly in the outpouring of the Spirit and the fall of Jerusalem (assuming 9:27 is to be taken this way). The casting out of demons is a sign of its presence (11:20). The royal power of God requires obedience and self-surrender if its blessings are to be experienced. Only those who persist in serving God are 'worthy' of the experience of God's power (9:62). In the ministry of Jesus and His apostles the kingdom 'draws near' (10:9, 11) and 'comes upon' (11:20) those to whom they minister. The kingdom is to grow. Disciples pray for its coming (11:2).

4. **To experience the ministry of two of the seventy-two disciples is to be challenged with a great and serious responsibility**. Jesus is with the pairs of disciples so that to come under their ministry is to have contact with Jesus Himself. Any town that rejects the pair of Jesus' co-workers will be in a position of intensified condemnation, and in a worst plight than wicked Sodom which was destroyed by God's fiery judgement from heaven (10:12).

Picking up the last point from verse 12, Luke 10:13–15 speaks of the terrible danger the Galilean cities are in because they had ample opportunity to learn from Jesus. The Galilean towns of Corazin and Bethsaida may not have been as wicked as the disgustingly evil town of Sodom, but then Sodom never had the privilege of having Jesus and His disciples minister to them. The Galilean towns have had great privileges, but this in itself brings them into a position of heightened responsibility.

Jesus Himself is represented by the seventy workers (10:16), so much so that to reject them is to reject Jesus Himself. To hear Jesus' Word and experience Jesus' power, in the ministry of one of Jesus' disciples, is to be confronted with Jesus Himself.

Note

1. We leave aside Luke 11:17, 18 which does not refer to God's kingdom.

Chapter 44

Rejoicing in God's Sovereignty

(Luke 10:17–24)

'The kingdom of God is ... joy in the Holy Spirit', said the apostle Paul (Romans 14:17). At this crucial point in the story, many people in Israel are hearing of God's kingdom. Jesus and His disciples are full of joy in the Holy Spirit.

1. **The disciples rejoice in their success**. The seventy-two disciples return from their mission full of joy. They have experienced many blessings, the greatest of which is the experience of seeing evil spirits leave the people when the disciples give a word of command (10:17).

2. **Jesus rejoices over Satan's defeat**. Jesus is also rejoicing. He has perceived in His own heart that Satan is losing his influence and power ('falling from heaven') as the disciples have done their work (10:18). Luke 10:18 is one of many passages that say that Satan is ruined by the ministry of Jesus. 'The great dragon is thrown down' (Revelation 12:9). Like the king of Babylon, he has 'fallen from heaven' (Isaiah 14:4, 12; compare Luke 10:15). He is 'cast out' (John 12:31) and bound (Revelation 20:1–3; the interpretation is of course disputed). He may be crushed under the feet of Christians (Romans 16:20). This defeat takes place in the ministry of Jesus and His disciples (see also Luke 11:20). They have authority over snakes (10:19); the 'snakes' and 'scorpions' are a piece of picture language referring to spiritual forces of darkness. The humblest Christian has authority to fulfil God's will; Satan cannot withstand any believer acting in the name and will of Jesus.

However Jesus gives the disciples a word of warning (10:20). They are not to rejoice over their work; they are to rejoice over their relationship to God. Their names are written in heaven, and it is that which is to be their supreme joy.

3. **Jesus rejoices over God's choice of the disciples**. On the same occasion, Jesus is given delight and satisfaction in the Holy Spirit, because of another aspect of the matter. The disciples are humble, ordinary people. Yet God has greatly used them. Jesus thanks His Father for them (10:21a). *'You have hidden these things from the wise and understanding and have revealed them to babes'*, He says (10:21b). There is a doctrine of predestination here. God is not obliged to reveal Himself to anyone. He can leave us as we are and so allow the blessings of His kingdom to remain hidden from us. When anyone comes to faith and understanding it is because of God's pleasure in the way He reveals Himself, and God chooses the most despised kind of people, the poor and the foolish. *'Has not God chosen the poor?'* (James 2:5) There are a few exceptions (Paul said 'Not many' in 1 Corinthians 1:26; he did not say 'Not any'). Yet generally the rich and the clever are left aside. Jesus rejoices that the conceited and proud are left aside. If the rich and clever experience God's kingdom at all they have to 'glory in their humiliation' (James 1:10).

4. **Jesus rejoices in His position as God's Saviour**. The previous thought leads Jesus on to make a statement about Himself. *'All things have been given to me by my Father . . .'* (10:22). The Father alone has supreme knowledge of Jesus, His Son, and it is the Father who reveals Jesus (10:23a). The Son alone has supreme knowledge of God the Father, and it is Jesus God's Son who reveals God to us (10:23b). It is a very rich statement concerning Jesus. (i) Jesus is God's Mediator and Representative. Every plan and purpose of the Father has been put into the hands of Jesus. With His power is all authority to reveal God, all control and mastery of everything in heaven and earth, all judgement, all power over the entire human race to give eternal life to the Father's chosen ones. (ii) The person of Jesus is so profoundly deep and mysterious no one but God understands Him or can reveal Him. (iii) The same thing is true the other way round. The person of God – the Father – is so profoundly deep and mysterious that no one but Jesus understands Him or can reveal Him. Jesus is the one

who fulfils the Father's plan of predestination. Only those 'to whom the Son chooses to reveal God' ever come to know God.

The Father and the Son together have a mutual knowledge of each other that no one else in the universe has. The Father and the Son are participants in the divine incomprehensibility and mystery. The Father and the Son are equally participants in a predestined plan of salvation. They give support to each other. The Father reveals the Son to God's chosen ones; the Son reveals the Father to God's chosen ones. They share the same mysterious nature; they accomplish the same mysterious plan.

5. **Jesus rejoices that His days are days of fulfilment**. *'Blessed are the eyes which see the things you see . . .'* (10:24). For many centuries God had been announcing that one day He would come as the King to His world. Prophets and kings had longed to see this day, but now it is here. Satan has fallen from heaven. Salvation is opened up for anyone to whom the Father reveals Jesus. The disciples have a privilege that has never been given to any generation previously. They are the first to experience the fall of Satan from his position of authority. The power of God's kingdom is already working; the message of salvation is already being preached. The kingdom has arrived! Great blessings were made known to kings and prophets. David and Abraham and Elijah had rich experiences of God. But the humblest Christian may have experiences of God in Jesus Christ which go further than anything known before the days of Jesus. The way into the holy of holies is made open.

Chapter 45

The Good Samaritan

(Luke 10:25–37)

Twenty-one of Luke's twenty-seven parables are found in Luke's 'travel narrative' (9:51–18:14). Sixteen of them are unique to Luke, including the famous 'Good Samaritan' and the 'Prodigal Son'.

1. We have first **an important question**. An expert in the Jewish law asks a question. He is not very sincere. He simply wants to find out whether Jesus is capable of handling tricky questions. It is a question about 'inheriting eternal life' (10:25). Yet it is an important question and Jesus answers it for the benefit of His disciples.

It is important to realise that 'inheriting eternal life' is not the same as 'justification by faith'. When a pagan man asks 'What shall I do to be saved?' we can simply say 'Believe on the Lord Jesus Christ'. Justification is 'without the law' (Romans 3:21).

But 'inheriting eternal life' is a bigger matter than simply one's initial experience of salvation. It is a larger matter than being 'justified'. Inheritance is reward. It is fully reaping the benefits of salvation. This lawyer is not asking a question about 'justification by faith'. His question really means: what must I do to get everything that God wants to give me? The man takes it for granted that this will involve doing, and Jesus does not contradict him, for Jesus only speaks about 'doing' (10:28, 37).

2. Next we have **an important method of answering a question**. *'What is written . . . ?'* asks Jesus (10:26), or *'How do you read?'* Jesus wants the man to answer for himself and He wants to encourage the man to get the answer from the

Scriptures. Jesus often does this. Our teaching must come from the written Scriptures.

3. Then we have **a wonderful answer**. Which part of the law would we quote in answer to the question: what must I do to enter into everything God has for me? There is not much in the law that you can quote at all in answer to this question. Actually the Mosaic law when it was first given on Mount Sinai scarcely spoke about love. It does once talk about loving God (Exodus 20:6) and there are two verses that say that we should love our neighbour (Leviticus 19:18, 38) and Moses referred to loving God (Deuteronomy 5:10; 6:5; 7:9; 10:12, 19; 11:1, 13, 22; 13:8; 19:9; 30:6, 16, 20) when he was preaching forty years after the first giving of the law.

This man is seeing something very profound about the law. He is seeing exactly what Paul said when he wrote Romans 13:8–10. There is much legislation in the Mosaic law, but for the Christian disciples one regulation is the key to everything else. The law points **in the direction** of love. There are about two thousands verses of legislation in the law but this lawyer was sufficiently discerning to see that the law is taking steps in the direction of love.

4. Jesus says that **the practise of love will lead to life**. 'Do this and you will live!' said Jesus. When the Old Testament says this it refers to national life. But I believe that when Jesus says these words He is referring to something more personal. Love leads to life! – to liveliness, vigour, energy, mobility of action. Love is invigorating because it gives a clear conscience.

None of this has anything to do with 'justification by faith'. Jesus is assuming that the person who is to show love is one who believes in Him. He is going **further** than answering a question about how we first step into our earliest experience of the kingdom of God. 'Inheriting eternal life' refers to entering into everything that God wants to give us. It is the practise of love that will lead to our laying hold of eternal life.

5. This conversation leads into the famous parable of the good Samaritan. It is well-known. A man is badly injured; he could die at any moment (10:30). Two highly respected religious experts come by, a priest and a Levite (10:31–32). They keep well away. They do not want to get involved with

the time-consuming needs of an injured person. It might be dangerous; the robbers might still be around. It will be expensive for them financially. It will have repercussions for them for a long time ahead.

A Samaritan comes by. Samaritan religion was corrupt. They were famous for idolatry. For many centuries they had a rival temple on Mount Gerizim. Jews hated them and despised them. As Jesus tells His story one can imagine a kind of shudder of horror as he says *'a Samaritan, as he was travelling, came to that very spot where the injured man was lying on the ground . . . '* (10:33).

'Now, Mr Lawyer,' says Jesus, 'Mr Expert-in-the-Scriptures, you have just talked about loving God and loving your neighbour. But you have got to do it! You have got to actually live out what you yourself have just said is the secret of entering into the inheritance of the kingdom of God.'

What was so wonderful about this Samaritan? He had no religious qualifications. He had no theological qualifications. He had nothing to commend himself in the eyes of the average Jew. The Samaritan did not run away from a situation of need. He looked. He felt compassion. He decided he would have to get involved. He did what needed to be done. He sacrificed something of his own comfort. He took upon himself a commitment that would give him some trouble in the future. His love touched his finances.

Jesus asks a question: *'which of these three . . . proved to be a neighbour?'* The answer was obvious. *'Go and do likewise'*, says Jesus. What is needed for the Christian to enter into everything God has for him? It is being like the good Samaritan. Religious professionalism will not achieve much. Compassionate love will lead into the experience of reaping the kingdom of God.

Chapter 46

One Thing Is Needful

(Luke 10:38–42)

From time to time we have reminders that Jesus is on a journey. This incident was one of many that took place 'as they were travelling along'. Jesus and His disciples were welcomed into the home of Martha. From other references to Martha we know that the place is Bethany. There is reason to think that Jesus was wandering around a lot at this time; this was a time when He was travelling near Jerusalem.

We meet two sisters, Martha and Mary. We know from John's Gospel that they had a brother, Lazarus, but he is not mentioned in Luke 10. One gets the impression here that Martha is the owner of the house: *'a woman named Martha received him'* (10:38).[1] It is obvious that Martha and Mary have different temperaments. Martha is a conscientious person. She seems to be the older sister. She wanted to show her love for Jesus by doing as much for Him as she could. Evidently she was a person of great activity, and was the kind of person who is not afraid to speak out her mind when necessary.

Mary is different. She shows her love for Jesus by wanting to listen to Him. She wants to listen rather than to speak, to sit rather than to rush around getting things done. She was an altogether different kind of person. It is important in the Christian life to accept the fact that personalities are different. We do not have to criticise other people because they are noisier than us or quieter than us. Some Christians will be very active and energetic. Others will be quieter and more contemplative.

Each temperament has its own weaknesses. One problem for the active and energetic person is that he or she tends never to sit still to listen to Jesus. Let us consider the three characters: Mary, Martha and Jesus.

1. **Consider Martha**. She is obviously a spiritually minded person. She appreciates Jesus and is hospitable towards Him. She puts herself to a lot of trouble to make Him feel welcome. But she is so busy in the work of the house that Martha is not listening to Jesus' teaching at all. She is busy in the home getting things in the house quite perfect for Jesus. Perhaps she is cooking for Him and His disciples. Perhaps she is making arrangements for His sleeping there that night.

She is a spiritual lady but her priorities are not right. There are some things more important than perfect housekeeping. Jesus actually only has a few weeks to live. He is making His last journey to Jerusalem. Martha is an active, energetic person. She gets busy in the things of the house, and is doing many things for Jesus but she is not giving much time to Jesus Himself.

Martha is a spiritual lady but she has fallen into perfectionism – the desire to get everything absolutely perfect. A desire for perfection in lesser things is a weakness of personality, not a strength. Life is too momentous to be worrying about perfect arrangements in minor matters. Martha gets quite distracted. She does not have much help. She has a lot to do and she gets distressed and anxious about how she will provide hospitality for Jesus and His friends. Eventually she is distressed and feels she must speak to Jesus. She wants Jesus to rebuke her sister, and get her to give her some help.

2. **Consider Mary**. Mary is not paying much attention to the work of the house. Jesus has a few disciples with Him and spends a lot of time teaching them. Mary joins them and sits at Jesus' feet listening to His teaching (10:39). She is ready to spend time with Jesus. Others things can be done later and do not have to be perfect in their arrangements.

3. **Consider Jesus**. At this point He commends Mary not Martha. He has a sense of priorities. Jesus had far more important things to attend to than to have perfect cooking arranged for Him. He was not wanting large and perfectly

prepared meals. Sometimes the travelling preacher is given more food than he wants. The Marthas of this world can be a nuisance! People love to be kind but sometimes they want to be kind in **their** way and so they end up being a nuisance. Kindness in such a situation is to attend to the visitor with the minimum of fuss and bother. Kindness is to listen to his message and give him time to pray and think.

Jesus speaks frankly to Martha. *'Mary has chosen the better part, and it is not going to be taken away from her'* (10:42). The one thing that is needful is to spend time listening to Jesus. Our earthly responsibilities require attention but not so much attention that we neglect to spend time with Jesus. We can risk being less-than-perfect in many areas of life but we must not be neglectful when Jesus is speaking. The housework can be done at any time; the voice of Jesus comes at special times and in those special times we must give our attention to Him.

One of the great secrets of the Christian life is to learn to put everything aside occasionally in order to listen to Jesus. It might be housework that gets left aside, it might be sermon-preparation! It is not needful to have a perfectly tidy home, and it is not needful for a preacher to have a perfectly tidy sermon! One thing is needful absolutely and utterly: it is necessary that when Jesus wants to teach us that we stop to listen to Him.

Note

1. Some manuscripts have the words 'into her house' but the better manuscripts lack these words.

Chapter 47

How To Pray

(Luke 11:1–13)

More than any other gospel, Luke's Gospel is about prayer (see my remarks in chapters 18, 22 and 40).

1. The disciples realise **the importance of prayer** (11:1–2). They have observed Jesus' praying, and it makes them realise that they need help in the matter of prayer, so they put a request to Jesus: *'Lord, teach us to pray, as John taught his disciples'* (11:1). It is interesting to note that John also made prayer a major part of his life. It is also worth noting that prayer can be taught. Yet we observe how Jesus gave teaching about prayer. In what follows (11:2–13) He does not say much about the externalities of prayer, the posture or place or the type of language that should be used. He does not say much about the gift of tongues (nor does He anywhere in the gospels). Tongues is a gift of the Spirit, and I pray in tongues myself, but we must not exaggerate its importance. Jesus never said much about it. The prayer He talked about was comprehensible and had definite content. He spoke mainly about what we should pray for (11:2–4), the character of true prayer (11:5–10), the willingness of God to hear us (11:11–12) and the greatest gift to pray for (11:13). This was His idea of teaching people to pray.

2. Jesus gave the disciples **a model prayer** (11:2–4) **in order to give them an idea of what to pray for**. Luke's version is shorter than Matthew's (Matthew 6:9–13) and Matthew's version might also be an abridgement of what Jesus said. Clearly He told them what to pray for, by giving them an example of what to pray for. As generally in the gospels, the written version is simply a summary.

What then should be the main content of our praying? It begins with the realisation of who it is that we are praying to (*'Father . . . '*). We begin by fixing our attention on God.

Our prayers are asking for things that God wants as well as things that we want. We are to make requests about His name (*'Your name be sanctified'*) and His kingdom (*'Your kingdom come'*).

Then we are allowed to ask for things that we need. We put to God requests in connection with our physical sustenance (*'Our bread . . . give us'*), our past sinfulness (*'Forgive us . . . '*) and our future strength (*'and do not lead us into temptation'*). This last request is not a request that we shall never be tempted. Rather it is a prayer that we might never be brought into a situation where we cannot stand. We ask not to be brought 'into' temptation, into a situation where we are likely to fail the test and fall into sin.

3. Jesus is next led on to speak of the greatest need in our praying. He gives a parable about **persistency in prayer** (11:5–10). Imagine, He says, that you are in a situation of serious need. A visitor arrives at your home and (in accordance with the courtesy of many parts of the world), you are obliged to feed the newly arrived visitor but you need some bread. So at midnight you go to your friend who lives nearby (11:5). You explain to him your problem, calling to him from outside the house (11:6). The nearby friend calls back from his bed where he is half-asleep. 'Don't bother me at this time of night,' he says. 'The children are with me in bed. I don't want to disturb them' (11:7). But the caller at the door goes on asking and asking, pleading that he is desperate and needs help. Finally the man inside gets up and helps him. Jesus comments (11:8), 'It was not friendship that made the man in bed get up and do something.' It was the 'importunity' – the shameless persistence – of the person asking for help that led to his getting an answer.

It is only a parable and it is only making one point. It is not saying that God is not a good friend, or that God is half-asleep. The only point of the parable is that persistence wins an answer! Jesus goes on to say: *'Ask . . . seek . . . knock'* and promises that we shall be heard (11:9–10), and that what we shall be given will be good (11:11–12).

4. The **basis of confidence** is the goodness of God. Even sinners have enough goodness in them so as to be able to give good things to their children. Will God not do even better? He is a good Father and when we come to Him making it clear what we need, by persistent steady praying, He will give to us an abundance of good things.

5. The **greatest gift** for which we should pray is the gift of the Holy Spirit: *'. . . how much more will the heavenly Father give the Holy Spirit to those who ask Him!'* (11:13). It is not a reference to praying for the Day of Pentecost. Nor does it precisely refer to praying for the baptism with the Spirit. It is rather a prayer that disciples – ourselves included – ought to be praying all the time. The disciples needed the help of the Spirit. They had work to do for Jesus and they needed the constant daily empowering of the Spirit. Even before the abundant outpouring of the Spirit that came on the day of Pentecost, the Spirit was working in the disciples, and they could ask for more of His working in their lives.

Such praying is still needed in the life of the modern Christian. Even mighty spiritual experiences do not cancel out the need to go on praying for the work of the Spirit. Every time we minister for Jesus, every time we tell others about Him, every day we go out to work, we need to pray, 'Lord give me Your Holy Spirit.' And the Father will hear the praying of His children.

Chapter 48

Deliverance

(Luke 11:14–26)

At some time in His travels, Jesus compelled a demon causing dumbness to leave a suffering man or woman (11:14). The crowds were amazed, but some maintained that Jesus had power over demons only because He was a servant of the devil (11:15). It was, they said, a demonic miracle. People who say they believe in the miraculous, but are then confronted with the miraculous, may well attribute the events they see to Satan. Many movements of the Holy Spirit have at first been attributed to Satan.

There were also people around who said they needed a sign of their own choosing, performed at their command and at their timing, before they would believe in Jesus (11:16). Jesus had done many miracles, many 'signs', but these were not enough for the critics. They wanted a sign specially laid on for them!

Jesus first responds to the claim that He is demonically empowered (11:17–26). Later He will reply to the request for a sign (see 11:29–32).

1. **The test of a spiritual kingdom is the direction it is moving in**. A kingdom or a family, says Jesus, which is internally divided will achieve nothing. Disunity is fatal (11:17). It is this principle that applies to Satan's kingdom (11:18). A man or a woman has just been **delivered** from Satan. Is Satan working against himself? Surely not. There were 'exorcists' in Israel, believing people who were used by God in this way. They were well-known to the people of Israel. Jesus says, 'ask them!' (11:19). The well-known and apparently well-recognized 'exorcists' in Israel will tell the Pharisees: Satan does not bring

deliverance! The best proof that God is at work is when it is obvious that Satan's kingdom is being opposed. Satan will not cast out Satan, so when we see sin and Satan being put down we may know God is at work. On the other hand, no amount of excitement proves anything if the long-term results do not show any signs of the power of sin and Satan being repelled.

2. **Exorcisms are a proof of God's kingdom**. Jesus says, *'If it is by the finger of God that I cast out demons then the kingdom of God has come upon you'* (11:20). Demon possession is a fact. Some people seem to enjoy the fact; they see demons everywhere! Any time they visit a congregation anywhere they want to practise a 'deliverance ministry'. Personally, although I believe that demons are real and I believe that deliverance is real, yet a lot of what is called 'deliverance ministry' does not seem to me to be the real thing. I cannot see much evidence of Satan's kingdom being driven back by many of those who claim 'deliverance ministries' in our own days. After such people have gone, there seem to be more problems to handle than before they came, and the pastor has to sort out the mess! But still, demon possession is a fact! Real deliverance, not the 'playing' kind is a sign of the presence of God's power. The kingdom of God is here! Wherever Jesus is working there God's kingdom – His royal power – is at work.

3. **The work of Jesus is to bind Satan**. The devil is like a strong man in a castle guarding his possessions (11:21). He can be defeated only by superior power, but Jesus is the one who has that superior power. Jesus is 'the stronger One' (11:22). The result of the work of Jesus is release from Satan. We must notice that the work of Jesus comes first. After He has acted in power the 'possessions' of Satan are released. It is obvious that the 'possessions' are people; it was a person who was released according to Luke 11:14.

The 'plunder' of Satan is taken out of the castle and distributed. The parabolic detail must not be pressed too hard but it clearly refers to the way in which lives are radically changed after Jesus has been at work. People see the evil of sin and they reject sinful and wicked ways radically. They call upon God for mercy; they get close to God. They become zealous in serving God, they lose their obsession with worldly pleasures.

The battle between Satan and Jesus is a strong one. No one can be neutral in the presence of Jesus. *'Whoever is not with me is against me'*, says Jesus. The Christian gospel is a conflict, and there are only two sides in the battle (11:24). Satan's kingdom, in any particular area of life, is either going forward or backward. Any person is either getting increasingly entangled in sin or he is getting released from sin. The people who have accused Jesus of having demonic power (see 11:15) in fact are themselves part of Satan's possessions and are being held fast by him.

There is another danger that Jesus warns of. When Jesus is at work deliverance from demons can take place without conversion. An evil spirit can leave but then return to the 'empty house' of an unconverted person's life (11:24–26). In which case 'the last state of that person is worse than the first'. Deliverance from demons must be followed by true conversion. There are degrees of wickedness. A temporary 'deliverance' from wicked ways, if not followed by true conversion, has no lasting value. This is the explanation of many who 'fall away' from what they claim has happened in their lives. But they were not 'falling away' from a life indwelt by the Holy Spirit; they are 'falling away' from a life that is 'swept and put in order' but not inhabited! Having escaped entanglements of Satan they are entangled again and are overpowered. Reformation without conversion is of no value. We have to have Jesus in our life before we are safe from Satan.

Chapter 49

Recognising Jesus

(Luke 11:27–36)

Jesus needs to reply to the demand for a sign (11:16). An opportunity came when a woman spoke warmly about Him. How wonderful it must be, she said, to be the mother of Jesus (11:27). Jesus replies.

1. **Relationship to Jesus does not come by physical descent.** Not even the 'virgin Mary' (as she is often called) had any spiritual relationship to Jesus, except by her faith and her obedience.

2. **Two ingredients are needed if we are to have a close relationship to Jesus**: (i) hearing Him and (ii) obeying Him (11:28). They are quite distinct. The gospels constantly make the point that it is necessary to hear Jesus' voice. Some never hear the voice of Jesus. But even after one has heard Jesus, that is still not the end of the matter. The response is not automatic. Close relationship to Jesus comes not by the spiritual experience of knowing He is speaking to us; it comes at the point where we obey Him. 'Blessed are those who hear the word of God and keep it'.

When the crowds became larger (11:29) Jesus took up the matter of the request for a sign. There is a link between 11:27–28 and 11:29–36. Jesus wanted people to take heed to His word. They were not so interested in His word, but wanted preliminary signs. The word was not enough for them.

1. **Jesus Himself is the sign**. No sign will be given, says Jesus, except *'the sign of Jonah'* (11:29). The kind of sign they want will not be given at all. God does not gives 'signs' at the demand of unbelieving people. The only sign will be Jesus Himself risen from the dead. Jonah came to the people of

Nineveh as someone delivered from death (11:30). In the same way, the proof that Jesus is who He says He is will be the resurrection. Jesus will come to them as one back from the dead. Through His apostles empowered by the Spirit, He will come to them like Jonah, preaching repentance. This is the only sign they are going to get! It will not come in such a way as to force them into anything; faith will still be required. The visible appearances of the risen Jesus will be to His disciples. Believers will have their doubts assisted. Unbelievers will not get the kind of proof they want; they will face the Word of God.

Similarly Solomon was a sign to his generation. It was Solomon himself who was a hint to the queen of Sheba that God was at work in Israel (11:31). In Jesus, God was doing something far greater.

2. **The nearness of Jesus is a great privilege** (11:31–32). The example of the Queen of Sheba (see 1 Kings 10:1–13) will be a great condemnation to the men of Jesus' day (11:31). She was a Gentile woman who lived hundreds of miles away from Israel, yet took great effort to investigate what God was doing in Solomon. But these men of Jesus' day have Jesus in their midst but are not ready to hear Him. The pagan Assyrians of Jonah's day were willing to listen to Jonah, but the people who have had so many privileges – the Jews – wish to find ways of evading the Word of God (Jesus still has in mind the events of 11:15, 16). In the judgement day the example of the Ninevites will arise to condemn the Jews listening to Jesus' voice. People were impressed with 'the sign' of Jonah. They were impressed by 'the sign' of Solomon. Why should they not attend to Jesus. He is God's sign; God will not answer their demands in any other way.

3. **God wants Jesus to be recognized**. No one brings a light into a house but then hides it in a cellar or under a 'bushel' (a measure for measuring grain). Jesus is the light; God wants the light to be seen (11:33). Yet light requires sight. God has given the light, but do they have eyes to see? (11:34).

Jesus uses an illustration. The 'eye' (11:34) is the ability to recognise Jesus. In ordinary life 'the eye is the lamp of the body'. If you can see clearly you are able to move around with ease. You do not stumble against unseen objects. But if the eyesight is damaged and you are unable to see, it affects every aspect of life. Your whole body is full of darkness. You stumble against unseen things around you. You are unable to walk very far. The clear-seeing eye is the key to ease of movement for the whole body. So it is with Jesus. Recognition of Jesus is the key to the whole of life. Many of these people talking to Jesus were proud of their religion, and yet they were unable to recognise the Son of God who was living among them.

Jesus gives a warning. 'Be careful lest the light in you be darkness'. Many people listening to Jesus felt that they were spiritually enlightened; they felt that they had 'the light'. But even their so-called 'light' was in fact darkness.

4. **Jesus invites them to total illumination**. If they will recognise Him, if they will truly hear His voice, they will be enlightened indeed. It will be like receiving eyes with totally clear vision. It will be like being a clear-sighted person in a brightly lit house. Everything will come clear.

Clear vision in life comes by recognising Jesus. He gives true understanding. He gets us to see everything the way it truly is. People without Jesus are stumbling in the darkness. They do not really understand life. They do not even understand themselves. Only when our whole body is full of light, do we see things as they really are.

Chapter 50

Religious or Christian?

(Luke 11:37–54)

A Pharisee asked Jesus to dine with him (11:37) and is astonished to notice that Jesus did not keep the Pharisees 'oral tradition' concerning hand-washing before meals (11:38). Jesus did not bother about man-made additions to the law of Moses. Hand-washing before meals was not simply a matter of hygiene; it was a religious ritual. Ritualistic regulations had become so traditional that 'religious' people in Jesus' day kept them. There were rules about how much water should be used, and how it should be done.

Jesus was not a very 'religious' person. He loved God, but He was not concerned to keep a multiplicity of regulations about how to eat food!

1. **Traditional religion worries more about externalities than the state of the heart**. It is **inner** cleanliness that is needed (11:39). One can be religious on the outside and yet have a lot of greed and malice and insincerity within one's heart. God is the creator and Lord of every aspect of life (11:40). The heart means more to Him than external religiousness. What is needed is love towards people (11:41). The Pharisees were actually a very greedy people; it is surprising how often religious people want plenty of money! If the Pharisees will overcome their greed for money and start being generous to the needy, then their inner heart will be clean (11:41). The whole of life will be 'clean' for them. They will enjoy all of God's creation and partake of food with gladness and generosity. Ritual washing will be unimportant, a matter of hygiene perhaps but nothing more.

2. **Traditional religion is often worried about burdensome legislation but neglects bigger matters** (11:42). The Pharisees would be extraordinarily strict about tithing! They were very fussy about counting out every bit of green mint to give one tenth to God. They were very diligent about 'tithing' the garden herb called 'rue', and every other kind of edible herb but they neglected the bigger demands of life. The Pharisees were very happy about **this** aspect of religion. It is surprising today how many preachers love to preach about tithing but rarely preach about justice or love! Walk into the average church or put on a typical 'Christian video-tape' and you are likely to be getting a sermon about tithing, but you are not very likely to be hearing a message about justice!

The Pharisees loved praise from other people (11:43) but were like concealed tombs (11:44), a grave dug in the ground filled with the bones of the dead. Such a grave might be unmarked. A Pharisees might walk over one by mistake and get 'defiled' by contact with the dead. Jesus says that it is the Pharisee who is the source of defilement. If others come into contact with a Pharisee they are likely to get defiled by the hypocrisy of this kind of religion.

One of the experts in the law protests at what Jesus says (11:45), but Jesus insists on the truth of what He says. The Pharisees require others to accept heavy regulations, but it was noticeable (as it is still) that legalistic preachers do not always live up to the demands they press on others (11:46).

3. **Traditional religion admires the past but is not willing for God do anything today**. The Pharisees claim to admire yesterday's spiritual heroes but there is no one that they recognise as having a word from God for today! For **today's** preachers and ministers they only have criticism. Pharisaism is still with us! There are plenty of traditional Christians who admire yesterday's heroes but persecute today's champions of faith (11:48).

4. **Traditional religion always persecutes true faith** (11:49–51). Jesus speaks of 'the Wisdom of God' (11:49). It is a way of indirectly referring to Himself (as is suggested by Matthew 23:34). He (as God's Wisdom in the flesh) will send prophets and apostles to His Church. They will be persecuted, but not

very far ahead will come God's judgement upon the city of Jerusalem (11:50–51). The long tradition of resistance to God has been tolerated for a long time. The first person in the Bible to die for real faith was Abel. He was killed by his brother Cain, but it should be noticed that Cain was a 'religious' man who brought an offering to God (Genesis 4:5). Zechariah was also killed by religious people who did not want to have God speak to them (2 Chronicles 24:22). Yet a time is coming, says Jesus, when all such religion will fall under God's judgement. He is indirectly predicting the fall of Jerusalem.

5. **Traditional religion is always resistant to God** (11:52). The men that Jesus was speaking to were experts in the law of Moses. Matthew 11:52 is a verse that could be applied to much modern biblical scholarship. Since the nineteenth century biblical scholars have, with some exceptions, been hindering men and women rather than helping them. The very scholars who are supposed to help people understand the Scripture actually lock people out of salvation. How often that has happened in the last two hundred years of biblical scholarship!

This time of Jesus' ministry was a turning-point. The religious leaders began doing everything they could to get Him to say something which they could use to have Him executed (11:53–54). So they were proving that what Jesus had said was true. They had religion but their hearts were full of hate.

We are half-way through Luke's Gospel and we would do well to ask ourselves a few questions. What sort of religion or Christian faith do we have? There is a religiosity that does no good for anyone at all. It is burdensome, legalistic, full of boring meetings and heavy regulations. Jesus the Son of God comes bringing forgiveness and joy, and lifts us into the joy and love of God. This does not come through 'religion; it comes through faith in Jesus.